EUGENE O'NEILL

A Poet's Quest

To My Wife

EUGENE O'NEILL

A Poet's Quest

BY

RICHARD DANA SKINNER

*With a correct chronology
of the O'Neill Plays
as furnished by
Eugene O'Neill*

NEW YORK
RUSSELL & RUSSELL · INC
1964

PRINTED IN THE UNITED STATES OF AMERICA

CONTENTS

v

Part Two — Regression

Part Three — Emergence

THE CHRONOLOGY OF THE O'NEILL PLAYS

When I asked Mr. O'Neill's permission to write about his plays "from the viewpoint of their inner continuity," it was agreed that he was not to see the manuscript of the book in advance of publication since it was important to have me form my own opinions of the poetic connection between the various plays by judging from their actual content, uninfluenced by any ideas Mr. O'Neill might have on the subject.

But he did realize that it would be equally important for me to know the actual sequence in the writing of the plays — as distinct from their production or publication dates — and with this in mind, he prepared a brief outline in letter form with dates and explanatory comments. His letter follows :

Whatever "inner continuity" there may be in these plays, I gladly leave to you to unravel — for whether I shall agree with you or not, after reading your comments, it is undoubtedly true that an author is not always conscious of the deeper implications of his writings while he is actually at work on them, and perhaps never becomes fully aware of all he has revealed.

Of course, some plays were written in one year, and re-written into their publication and stage-produced forms in a later year — usually, this meant only a condensation, without any change in essentials.

I enclose a list with dates and some explanatory comments which should make this clear to you.

1913-1914	Fall and Winter	The five one-act plays in "Thirst"
1914	Spring	"Bound East for Cardiff" (Very important from my point of view. In it can be seen, or felt, the germ of the spirit, life-attitude, etc., of all my more important future work. It was written before my work under Prof. Baker at Harvard)
1914-1915	Fall and Winter	Nothing of importance
1915-1916		Nothing
1916	Summer	Start of the Provincetown Players — wrote "Before Breakfast"
1917	Winter, at Provincetown	Wrote "In the Zone"—"Ile"—"The Long Voyage Home"—"Moon of the Caribbees"
1917	Summer	A short story (never published) about stokers containing the germ idea of "The Hairy Ape"—also an outline of the idea for "Beyond the Horizon"
1918	Winter Summer Fall	"The Rope"—"Beyond the Horizon"—"The Dreamy Kid"—"Where the Cross is Made" First draft of "The Straw"
1919	Winter Spring	"Chris"— never published, although produced by George Tyler outside of New York. This was the play from which "Anna Christie" developed. Final draft of "The Straw"

1920	Winter	"Gold"
	Summer	"Anna Christie"
	Fall	"Emperor Jones" and "Diff'rent"
1921	Winter	"The First Man"
	Spring and Summer	First draft of "The Fountain"
	Late Fall	"The Hairy Ape" (written in three weeks)
1922	Summer	Final draft of "The Fountain"
	Fall	One half of "Welded"
1923	Winter	Finished "Welded"
	Summer	Outline and one scene of "Marco Millions"
	Fall	"All God's Chillun Got Wings"
1924	Winter and Spring	"Desire Under the Elms"
	Summer	Finished "Marco Millions" in its original two part two-play form, each play short full length.
1925	Winter	Final draft of "Marco Millions," condensed into one play. "The Great God Brown"
	Fall	Half of a first draft of "Lazarus Laughed"
1926	Winter and Spring	Final draft of "Lazarus Laughed"— except for some cutting and condensing in 1927
	Spring and Summer	First half of "Strange Interlude"
1927	Winter, Spring and Summer	Final draft of "Strange Interlude"
1928	Spring and Summer	"Dynamo"
1929 to 1931		"Mourning Becomes Electra"

1932	Spring and Summer	First and second drafts of "Days Without End"
	September	"Ah, Wilderness"
	Fall	Third draft of "Days Without End"
1933		Final fourth draft of "Days Without End"

This letter from Mr. O'Neill has proved invaluable to me in tracing the inner connection between his plays and the gradual development of his poetic imagination.

RICHARD DANA SKINNER

PREFACE

This book is in no sense a series of dramatic reviews of Eugene O'Neill's plays. During the past ten years, I have reviewed most of his important plays in the weekly pages of *The Commonweal*, and in a book, *Our Changing Theatre*, I discussed many of these plays again from the purely dramatic view. But during all this period, I have become increasingly aware of a quality in the O'Neill plays above and beyond their theatrical significance — the quality of continuous poetic progression, linking them all together by a sort of inner bond. They have a curious way of melting into one another, as if each play were merely a chapter in the interior romance of a poet's imagination. This inner continuity now seems to me far more fascinating — and far more important, as a subject of literary criticism — than the dramatic merits of the individual plays. The following pages merely try, in a brief way, to trace this greater drama within many dramas.

Moreover, this book does not attempt any appraisal of the much discussed morality of the individual O'Neill plays. Many of them deal with highly "immoral" people, in the ordinary acceptance of that word. Some of the plays are unquestionably morbid. They might easily have an unhealthy effect upon sensitive or disturbed minds. But others represent an intense and passionate search for truth and for religious faith ; and this much can be said for nearly all of them, that they do not glorify the evil in men. O'Neill characters do not escape the consequences of their deeds. The proud are humbled or destroyed. The possessive lose the objects of their desire. The connection between evil and disaster is direct, internal as well as external, and, in the true dramatic sense, inevitable.

This frank recognition of the inherent destructiveness of evil is not enough, however, to settle the question of a play's morality or "decency." A moral ending does not, of itself, make a moral play — though it does create a play with a "good moral." The distinction is obvious. A play with a "good moral" may still be surfeited with objectionable dialogue, or with scenes so realistically descriptive of evil as to leave a most unfortunate impression on an audience or on a reader. Many spectacular motion pictures of recent years, for example, have made a "moral ending" the excuse for a lavish display of vice, including in one notable instance even perversion. Thus one finds a wide field for disagreement in any effort to discuss the morality or the "decency" of any individual play, and markedly so in the case of O'Neill's works.

But the poetic content of the O'Neill plays as a whole is a very different matter. Here the "moral" rather than the "morality" of the play becomes the important issue —

for in the "moral" we find the key to the poet's own feelings toward the characters of his imagination. If we were dealing with an insincere author, one willing or eager to exploit the pictorial presentation of evil, the case might be quite different. But O'Neill's work, from his earliest days, shows the hall-mark of integrity. He is an authentic dramatist and an instinctive poet. He writes in a veritable torrent of deep feeling from which his inner attitude toward his characters is clearly discernible at every stage. For this reason, the "moral" of his individual plays is the exact measure of his interior or spiritual progress as a poet. One might find deep encouragement from the moral of a given play and still believe, as a matter of personal judgment, that the dramatic treatment was needlessly brutal, or realistic, or lacking in mature restraint and taste. This means that one may sincerely welcome the inner theme of a play — as part of a larger sequence in the conflict of good and evil — without in any sense relishing the concrete dramatic form, or the details of plot, treatment, dialogue or realistic emphasis. I feel this brief explanation of viewpoint is clearly due those readers who might expect to find a type of discussion which is omitted for the distinct purpose of keeping theme and inner significance quite separate from external dramatic qualities.

For the rest, I can only emphasize the fact implied in Mr. O'Neill's letter to me under the heading "The Chronology of the O'Neill Plays," that the manuscript of this book was not submitted to Mr. O'Neill in advance of publication. It does not have his endorsement, even by implication. He may easily disagree with many of the poetic meanings I have attributed to his various plays. But this freedom in viewpoint and interpretation seemed to be the right way to approach a matter of such close personal concern to an author, and the only way to maintain full integrity of literary criticism.

PART ONE — *TURMOIL*

I

O'NEILL — THE POET OF THE INDIVIDUAL

THE plays of Eugene O'Neill have never seemed to be solely of the theatre. They have, as it were, followed one out into the noisy streets and into the privacy of one's room, into the greater privacy, even, of one's inner thoughts and feelings, and not for a few hours or days, but with a certain timeless insistency. They have become a part of the real world as well as the world of make-believe. They simply refuse to stay locked within the walls of the theatre. Nor, in this bursting of traditional bounds, do they confine themselves to one segment or another of realistic affairs. Bernard Shaw was once capable of writing a play that mixed itself up later on with the actual doings of Fabian socialists, and Ibsen wrote many plays that prompted clinical quests into actual heredity or made one speculate moodily about false pride and the social order. But neither Shaw nor Ibsen had the poet's gift of reaching to the emotional and moral inwardness of life without any relation to specific events, or times, or people. O'Neill has that gift in abundance. His plays are neither social sermons nor contemporary satire. They are more like parables.

Parables of course are dangerous weapons in the hands of a poet of real stature. They are enormously effective in implanting an idea, but the idea itself may be a false one, or those listening to the parable may apply it in many ways never intended by the teller of the tale. O'Neill's plays have suffered as parables, both from the confusion and variety of his own ideas and from the many interpretations audiences have read into them. As an individual poet, O'Neill has gone through countless phases of thought and emotion, many of them contradictory, and many of them tortured with alternating doubt and premature discovery of spiritual solvents. All of this has found expression in his plays and has carried through, for good or ill, to vast audiences. He has been accused of everything from charlatanism to extreme morbidity and immorality, and has been praised for everything from supreme tragic expression to profound philosophical insight. But there is another way to appraise and eventually to revere the O'Neill plays, and that is in their singular continuity as the expression of the immemorial "poet's pilgrimage"— as the representation in outer and objective form of certain elemental struggles and conflicts which were as much a part of the humanity and the poetry of China, Palestine and Greece as they are of the tumultuous life of our own day.

The poet lives a vastly larger life than the man. He lives to the utmost possibilities of human nature, both in good and in evil. He may be the summation of all virtues in his private life and yet experience in his poetic imagination the nadir of moral degradation. He may pass his entire life in a country village and yet encompass the catastrophe of an empire. His parables are not the outline of himself but the rhythm and splendor and often the terror of something far above and beyond his personal experience.

Eugene O'Neill has written many plays in which the material obviously results from the impact of personal experience — his early plays of the sea, for example. In other plays, a personal moral conflict is clearly indicated, not in the outer material but in the theme. Yet through all these plays, as well as through his more highly imaginative creations, there is a larger unity, almost like the movements of a symphony, which expresses the larger life of the poet as distinct from the personal life and problems of the man. It is this larger aspect of the O'Neill plays which has always seemed to be not merely of the theatre but also part of the great stream of poetic literature coursing through all history and legend. It follows, in many extraordinary details, a universal theme found in all deeply rooted folk-lore and in the innermost experiences of great mystics. In its simplest sense, it is the conflict of good and evil, a picture in objective form of the stretching and tearing of a soul between a will

toward the good and an appetite for the revolt of sin.   In
its deeper sense, it is the quest for a resolution of this
conflict and for ultimate peace.

Folk-lore, as the poetry of a race, abounds in examples
of this major theme.   The dragon or the beast must be
conquered before the peace of love can be achieved.   The
princess of legend is not content to let her knight languish
at her feet in an ecstasy of love.   A dragon is destroying
the countryside.   Her knight must go forth into the slime
and terrors of this reality outside before he can claim the
perfection of her love.   Often the dragon is a beast of
many heads and many lives, like the multiplicity of evil
to be conquered in the soul.   Again, we have the whole
series of legends, like Beauty and the Beast, in which the
struggle is not so much to conquer evil as to attain that
maturity which makes the fears and the monsters of youth
turn into instruments of peace and beauty.   A child is
allowed to grow up with a vague horror of sex, as something evil in itself, only to discover later that it can become the supreme physical expression of man's creative
impulses.   The "beast" can be won, through love and
understanding, to an end of beauty.   In still another
group of legends we have the fears of immaturity ap-
pearing as giants blocking the path to manhood.   The
Jacks must kill the giants of fear before the world is fit
to live in.   It is hardly necessary to delve into the intri-
cate theories of racial subconsciousness to see how univer-
sally mankind objectifies in legend and story the common

experiences and the terrifying inner struggles of the pilgrimage from tortured youth to peaceful maturity.

Poets are peculiarly sensitive to the almost infinite variations of this inner conflict. No matter how objective in detail the poet's story may seem, he is almost certain, in his major works, to catch up the fury and agony of the search for that ultimate virtue which will bring the warring elements into harmony. We find this in the wanderings of the Homeric heroes, in the Virgilian descent into Hades, in Dante's progress through the inferno and purgatory into a paradise filled with that love "which moves the sun and the other stars." We find it again in Milton, in Francis Thompson's *Hound of Heaven*, and in Richard Wagner's cycle of the Ring tragedy culminating in the exaltation of Parsifal. Blake found in his *Book of Job* another expression of the universal conflict and quest. Shakespeare was never a more universal poet than in probing the soul of the searching Hamlet. The Greek dramatists thought and wrote of little else than the fates, furies and conflicting obligations which beset every human action and decision.

In a still larger sense, the peoples of the earth have fought and lived almost as if they were acting out a poet's dream. They have reached a summit of achievement and discovered the pride that follows it only to sink again into blackness and despair and the terrors of a mighty purging. Greece, and the shadowy imitation of Greece that was Rome, fell into the dark night of Europe, to re-

awaken for a short period of incandescence in the thirteenth century. Then came pride of intellect in a new
form, the renaissance of a Greek culture that no longer
fitted the souls of men and the new terrors of the dark
age of science which was destined to last another five centuries. Science, which was to liberate man through his
own intellect, became the master instead of the servant.
Instead of exalting man, each new discovery, like a mystical increase in the "knowledge of good and evil," made
man smaller and smaller in his own eyes. It multiplied
his problems of good and evil a thousand fold. It threw
him into the wild and tortured confusion and savagery
that reached its first grotesque crisis in the great war.
Mankind finds itself today a chained Prometheus for
having brought the new fire of science to disrupt the soul.
The problem of humanity today, as the poet would feel
and describe it, is to discover the humility which can make
man master of his new science. A paradox — certainly,
but not a new one. It is Beauty and the Beast all over
again. It is not science that is wrong, but the pride with
which men have used science. It is men who have made
science their beast, and the beast can be transformed only
through a new humility among men themselves. It was
in Palestine that the words of a parable rang forth —
"he that humbleth himself shall be exalted." These
words were wholly forgotten when man proudly set out
to free himself through his scientific intellect alone.

It is because Eugene O'Neill is of the very stuff and

fibre of this age that his poetic intuitions are of immeasurable importance to us, as a reflection of what we are as individuals and as a rumor of what we may become. He is part of an age which, if we were not living in it ourselves and filled with the egotism of it, we would recognize as a darker night of civilization than the world has known for many long centuries. What man is there living, unless he be supernaturally inspired, who will tell you that he sees clearly the road ahead? The very multiplicity of our knowledge of detail has obscured our vision of the whole with a veil as black as midnight. Wars, conflicts, riots, revolutions, racial deities, sullen envy — are these the daylight of civilization, or rather the valley of the shadow of humanity's dreams?

O'Neill is not, in the accepted sense, a poet of his times. That is, he rarely attempts consciously to write of current conditions or problems. When he does, as in his play, "Dynamo," the result is not always happy, for he is not that rarest of all persons, a poet who is also a philosopher. But in the sense common to all poets, the problems which he objectifies in the characters of his plays are those of peculiar moment to the present day; and in an age that thought it had discarded morals, these problems turn out to be moral ones! It is precisely in this fact that his intuitions are probably far keener than those of the essayists and the philosophers. In an age that superficially deifies science and amorality, O'Neill is obsessed with questions of good and evil. In a world still given over to economic determinism, he writes of sin and retribution — and what he writes proves to be of absorbing interest to millions!

What O'Neill has done, after the historic fashion of poets, is to sense far in advance of the intellectualists a deep change in the currents of individual men's thoughts and emotions. In that curious super-life which the poet leads, which may be in almost absurd contrast with his actual life as an individual man, the hunger and pain and doubt of great masses of people may of course seem very personal. He finds himself fascinated with the titanic pride of such a man as Emperor Jones, and writes of his tragic downfall with perhaps little thought that he is prophesying the collapse of a whole era of proud individualists. Or, again, the incest problem of the old Greek plays becomes strangely urgent. It may never occur to him that incest is in one sense a symbol of self-worship and self-seeking, and that this has become the besetting sin of a generation that denies any power greater than humanity and so moves on to slow death through man's worship of mankind. The play is written as a story of individuals. But in the doom of its characters can be read the fate of nations.

Yet it would be a grave mistake to think of O'Neill chiefly as the poet of a social order in process of vast change. That would exaggerate the faint though discernible connection between his instinct for moral issues and the social characteristics of the day. He is, above all else, the poet of the individual soul, torn and warped, perhaps, by the surrounding mass currents, but still supremely the master of its individual choice.   The Ibsens and the Shaws have used individuals to express the problems of masses or of a social system.   Their characters have been almost passive victims of inheritance or of a convention or of mass view-point.   But with O'Neill, the problem of the individual as a soul in distress or torment has been clearly supreme.   It is the individual's rebellion against the mass, or his abject surrender to it that counts, rather than the action of the individual as representing the mass.   O'Neill as a poet does carry something of the force of a prophet in his writings, but in the sense that the achievements of his characters prophesy the types of individuals likely to be bred from the anarchy of our times rather than the mass types and the collective trends.

One might ask, for example, "are the days ahead of us apt to bring forth a new Francis of Assisi?" and hope to find a hint of the true answer in O'Neill's work.   But one could spend no end of futile days trying to discover a rumor of the typical business man or factory worker or politician or middle class householder of the next generation.   Looking backward, we can say that the long night of Europe did eventually produce a Saint Francis, a Dante, a Thomas Aquinas and a Leonardo da Vinci.   If we had lived in the tenth or eleventh centuries, we might have gathered this in advance from the poets of the day.   The troubadours of Provence, strangely enough, foreshadowed

not a little of the Franciscan idea of love. But to discover what the mass population of Europe was going to
be like, the poets would have helped us very little. In
the clear progressive unity of O'Neill's writings, we can
discover a great deal concerning certain rare individual
types likely to emerge from our discouraging present.
But to try to make a social philosopher out of him, as
some have tried, is to miss the whole point of his special
genius. He is the poet of the individual soul, of its
agony, of its evil will, of its pride, and its lusts, of its
rare moments of illumination, of its stumblings and grop-
ings in surrounding darkness, and of its superbly romantic
quest for deliverance through loving surrender.

II

O'NEILL'S EMERGING GENERATION

Before scanning the individual plays of O'Neill or attempting to trace their inner continuity, it is well worth while to examine more closely the emotional soil from which they have sprung and to separate its special from its universal qualities. The study of O'Neill is really an adventurous voyage into the inwardness of the American soul of yesterday and today. That soul must in the nature of events have a dual aspect, the first limited or inspired, as the case may be, by circumstances peculiar to American life and thought and emotions, and the second unlimited by either time or place and rooted in the universal experiences of mankind. Moreover, since we are dealing with poetic insight and intuition which penetrate far beneath outward symptoms, both aspects of the American soul as they are illuminated by O'Neill's work will inevitably take on a proportion and a sensitive vibrancy not easily recognizable in our ideas of mass psychology.

To put the matter somewhat differently, we are not concerned with average emotions nor with average perceptions. It would be utterly absurd, if we were examining the background of Plato or Aristotle, to waste much time in studying the average Athenian mentality of that day. A history of Greek wars and Greek politics throws very little light on why, at that particular time and place, two such towering mentalities should have reared themselves. But a study of Athenian poetry and of Athenian ideals would make the whole matter clear at once. The poets of Athens were not average Athenians, and the ideals of the Athenian state were the creations of leading men and not a spontaneous discovery of the Athenian masses. It is vastly to the credit of the Athenian people that they were willing and ready to absorb the ideals and tastes of their exceptional men, to enshrine the works of Praxiteles, to enjoy the plays of Sophocles and Euripides, to listen eagerly, if only for a short time, to the calm wisdom of Socrates, and to perpetuate and conserve the works of Plato and Aristotle. That is because the work of the sculptors and poets and playwrights and philosophers of Athens responded to deep and unexpressed human longings, because it was not the average taste or thought of Athens but something vastly above the average and thus worth an aspiring glance from those who could never reach the same heights.

The emotional scope of the average American soul in the last decade of the nineteenth century, when Eugene O'Neill as a boy was gathering his first sensitive impressions, was almost equivalent to that of a highly developed vegetable. It expressed itself rather well in brown-stone architecture, in golden oak furniture with flowery brass fittings, in a distaste for and a fear of fine music or sensitive literature, in a ready acceptance of sentimentality as a substitute for fervor, in admiration for rough physical prowess, in a love of convention for its own sake, and in an unquestioning acceptance of the superlative virtues of national heroes, past and present. But for all this slate-covered smugness of the average mood and temper, the nineties were strong and even splendid years once you glanced above the average.

One likes to recall, for example, the passionate love of fine music among those who refused to accept the current disdain for it. The very fact that the turn of a dial could not bring a symphony concert into the home meant that the only way to hear Beethoven or Liszt or Wagner was to be able to play an instrument, and to have studied music of the masters with something approaching consecration. In every city of reasonable size, you would find small but devoted and capable musical clubs, composed largely of amateur musicians whose intensive training had been little short of professional standards. They would be encouraged and guided in their work by brilliant members of that thinly scattered group of professionals who had found their way from Europe to American centers. In the most unexpected places you would discover a violinist who had come from Vienna with a European opera troupe or orchestra, only to find himself stranded when the troupe or orchestra went into bankruptcy. Or you might find a somewhat ancient opera soprano whose declining years were a bit ruefully given to teaching. These artists, stranded and otherwise, found a warm and eager reception in the few homes where their sterling musicianship was loved and understood. Musical gatherings in those days, with a mingling of amateur and professional, had much of the atmosphere of small European salons. There might be only two or three such homes in a dozen city blocks, but in those homes there was no mere polite "appreciation" of music. There was love and effort and intensity put into creative expression. One could not merely like music. One had to be a musician — and often an artist.

It was not wholly different with literature. One could buy books, to be sure, when one could not buy music at any price, save in one or two metropolitan centers. But good books were rare and to be discussed, read and reread, and cherished as part of a library that was an accumulation of real affection. Those bold enough to write anything other than fiction often needed the courage to finance the publication of their works, and had to feel amply repaid by the interest of a few hundred readers. But those were not days when every week brought forth "the most penetrating and masterly biography of the year." If an Orestes Brownson labored obscurely to bring new clarity to American philosophy, he at least did not have to compete for honors with several hundred young intellectuals who had mastered a pleasant journalistic style and dipped perilously into the latest psycho-

logical fads. In university towns, a philosopher like
Josiah Royce, whether he wrote or merely lectured, com-
manded not only the fruits of a reputation but also the
tribute of violent discussion. Style in writing was something which won honest admiration and the respect due
to any skilled craftsmanship. The very smallness of the
appreciative audience made for a sharpening of critical
judgment, a discrimination in praise and a lasting reputation, once it was won.

The nineties also had dignity — the dignity that comes
with a feeling for tradition as distinct from mere convention. The feeling toward furniture expressed this in a
curious way. In spite of the flood tide of golden oak
and of brass beds, there were many homes where ances-
tral pieces of colonial simplicity were quietly revered.
No one, except perhaps a few recent millionaires, ever
thought of calling these cherished pieces "antiques."
They were loved and given a place of honor because they
had belonged to a grandfather or a great-grandmother or
perhaps to some more distant ancestor who had made his
or her own small contribution to building American life.
They were a visible part of the accepted continuity
of family life. In homes that did not have a long
American background, there might be the equivalent pieces
of furniture brought from Germany after 1848, or a
musical instrument brought from Italy, or a memento
from a farm in county Sligoe or county Clare in Ireland.
You could not possibly think of something as "antique"

which had actually been used and perhaps prized by someone whose blood was still alive in you. And this dignity of inherited possession, this sense of continuous flowing life expressed in the feeling toward furniture, meant that the nineties were looking ahead as well as into the dim past. It was the dignity of those who have received life and feel they must pass it on to others. A sensitive person living in those days would have felt the obligation to create, quite simply and of course.

The opening years of the twentieth century, up to the outbreak of the world war, brought surprisingly little change in the average emotional content of American life. Its outward expression altered considerably, but not its inner nature. There was a certain lightening in taste as brown-stone architecture yielded place to decorative brick and white stone and as golden oak disappeared in favor of reproductions of colonial design. The advent of the automobile did bring people in touch with forgotten corners where outward simplicity had never been fully lost. But even the gradual perfection of artists' discs on the phonographs failed to undermine the antipathy to fine music and the fear of it bred of unfamiliarity. The iron rule of conformity in thought and attitude still dominated both parents and children. A sensitive boy of ten to fourteen with a secret hankering for artistic and imaginative values would have found himself practically outlawed by his companions, and regarded by their parents as distinctly queer or precocious. American life, once greatly stirred by the forming of a nation, and stirred again during and immediately after the Civil War, still found itself in the opening decade of the twentieth century lying fallow.   But ploughshares were at work.

The profound stirring of the subsoil which began about 1910 was much more than a direct premonition of the world conflict then brewing.   Something of the intensity of the life and love of art and of intelligent ideals among the isolated families of the nineties had begun to spread abroad.   The commonplaces of their existence became bit by bit the delighted discoveries of wider audiences, the somewhat wicked Bernard Shaw, the homeric Chesterton, the morbid and unsettling Ibsen, the thrillingly dangerous Russians, the puzzling Debussy, the sonorous and somewhat fearsome Wagner.   Then it happened by a curious coincidence that Theodore Roosevelt, the last relic of a day when hero worship could be substituted for creative thinking, prepared the path, quite unintentionally, which led a college president to the White House.   It was actually assumed by most youngsters of the nineties that only a military title had much chance of reaching the Presidency.   The "bloody shirt" of the Civil war and the only faintly spattered shirt of the Spanish war had become essential mantles for a popular leader. But once rough rider Roosevelt had stirred the social consciousness of the people, battered the trusts and dared to refer to certain wealthy giants as malefactors, the long emotional anaesthesia was at an end.   Even the average

American, much to his surprise, found himself eager to
listen to the literary cadences of Woodrow Wilson, a
college president with nothing more bloody and spectacular to offer than the advantages of historical culture
and soaring idealism.

By this time the universities were in a ferment.
Through a curious process of identification with the Presidency, they became more important in their own eyes and
correspondingly more aggressive. The student bodies
took to themselves a good deal of the new importance,
and broke forth into professional print astonishingly soon
after graduation or even before. The contagion spread.
Parents began to follow the lead of their children in the
new intellectual release, timidly at first, as if they could
not forget the philistine atmosphere of their youth, and
then with more vigor. A great deal of this ferment was
forced and not a little ridiculous. But it did serve the
purpose of lifting the ban against freer expression for the
few who possessed real talent or the rumors of genius.
Then came the war.

The average effect of the war is too well known to need
any comment. It stirred up all the astonishing contradictions that wars have always stirred up since the beginning
of time. But it did something that was neither average
in importance nor average in historical perspective. It
did something which no other war in history could possibly have done, because no other war in history had ever
been fought at the very culmination of a century of equal

scientific progress. The science that was to have liberated man turned on and crushed him, bombed him from the air, blew him to bits from beneath the sea, shattered him with steel or burned him to pulp with the arts of chemistry. With superb irony, it showed him the process of his destruction, horror after horror, in motion pictures. It placed his festering wounds under microscopes, the better to teach him the decay of all flesh. It analyzed into harrowing pieces his wavering and battle-shocked mentality. The materialism of a century turned to putrefying matter instead of into mastery. Man's scientific worship of mankind ended in millions of grinning skeletons disfiguring the face of the earth.

The war did something else, however, which other wars had done before, but which was still more than the average and tiresome effect of all wars. It brought the highly strung and re-sensitized youth of a new world into an almost mystical reunion with the older civilization from which it had sprung. The Crusades once did something like this for the youth of France, taking them in all their rough and scattered energy, in all their local pride and intolerance and in all their mixture of native and invader's blood and throwing them back into an older civilization to the East. When these late Crusaders left France, their country was still a turbulent outpost of Roman tradition. Even their churches, symbols of their highest glances, were covered with the low arches of Rome. But within fifty years after they returned from seeing the minarets of the East and discovering a unity with the source of their race, these now united men of France burst into a life that was astoundingly their own. Gothic towers rose from the churches of France, spears thrust heavenward, and with those towers the young men of France reared the civilization of the thirteenth century.

The great war may have done something like this to the mind and soul of America. We can not possibly be certain of it for many years to come. But we did have a race which, like the eleventh and twelfth century French, was a mixture of many bloods. We did have a rough and ready civilization which was as much an outpost of European culture as twelfth century France was an outpost of Rome. We had very little that we could call our own. Our music and our musicians were imported, and so was our literary standard. Our theatre, save for such indigenous products as Uncle Tom's Cabin and cheap melodramas, followed the European formulae. Our philosophy was a strange mixture of Rousseauism and of the English tradition which began with Hobbes. Only our energy was thoroughly native, and it lacked both direction and unity. The war threw a million or more of our young men directly back into the arms of the older civilization from which we had sprung. The end of the war threw these young men back again into every scattered county of the land, united for the first time in the memory of a common experience and capable, quite unconsciously, of becoming a leaven for new growth and original development. It is far too early to say whether or not this profound fact will bring forth in American life the present day equivalent of the thirteenth century civilization of France. If it does, we may expect a period of eager coordination of ideas, the outward symbol of new aspirations in an architecture wholly our own and a love of order marking the gradual maturity of a race after its adolescent period of childish individualism. The conditions precedent to such a transformation are clearly with us and very largely the outgrowth of that great migration of men east and then west again which was the sole positive contribution of the war.

We can at least point to many scattered bits of evidence that some such change is taking place. The familiar aftermath of all great wars has somewhat obscured the scene, but not wholly. There is nothing new nor startling in the decade of economic brutality that followed the war. It was a period of acute mental illness which we mistook for abounding health. The abysmal economic misery that followed was really the start of a mental convalescence. But it is very easy to overestimate the importance of both events. The truly important happenings escape our notice — the signs of a new spiritual hunger, the conscious effort to create order in our economic lives, the willingness to originate and not merely echo ideas, and the readiness to accept the discipline of leadership. Above all, we can see an eager curiosity to examine and appraise the old as well as the new and to accept what we believe to be good and true without prejudice as to its source or its age.

In science, for example, an Eddington of today can calmly upset the whole tower of materialism by saying that no informed scientist can continue to deny the possibility of freedom of the will! Our economists and political leaders are frankly adapting certain principles of the guild organization of industry and capital which flourished in the thirteenth century itself. Both new and old forms in literature are being combined with delightful freedom from prejudice. The infantile idea that forms must break entirely with the past to be truly worth while has completely broken down. The religious philosophy of a St. Thomas or of a St. Augustine is being studied eagerly on its own merits. As it is only two decades since their works were utterly ignored in our universities, it has been a major and startling discovery to many that St. Augustine built up a theory of evolution centuries before Darwin upset the Protestant fundamentalists. These mental attitudes and discoveries give us more than a hint that our American civilization may actually be emerging, as one might have hoped, into a boldly creative life of its own.

These changes in the American scene over the last fifty years are in no sense remote from Eugene O'Neill and his "poet's pilgrimage." They form an intimate part of him. As a true poet, he has clearly sensed most of them many years ahead of the rest of us. They contribute the special qualities to his work which make him peculiarly a mirror of the American soul in transition. They do not encompass the larger aspect of the poet's place in life, his response to universal mental and spiritual experiences. But they do affect the form in which he would express those larger experiences. They affect his choice of material and plot. They blend with and become part of the poet's consciousness and so lend to it their own color and flow of circumstance.

III

THE POET'S QUEST

THE preoccupation of Eugene O'Neill's plays with good and evil gives them at once their singular inner unity and their universal impact. Just as no European could have written these plays, because of their sensitive reflection of impending changes in American life and mood, so no European could fail to understand them, because they pass far beyond the limitations of the American scene and vibrate with the intensity of the universal life struggle. Had O'Neill merely mirrored back the American soul to itself, he would have remained a minor poet. But he has searched instead into the depths of the larger soul of mankind itself.

It would be exceedingly difficult to catch the deeper notes of O'Neill's work without attempting to understand the quality of some of those rich and terrifying inner experiences which the poets and mystics of all ages have tried to express. We might turn first to the saints, not because of their religion, but because they have been least thwarted psychologically in their ultimate quest, and because their experiences are well documented. They at least have passed beyond the turmoil of doubts and fears

and divided selves into something resembling a peaceful
unity of mind and soul.   They have actually moved from
inner discord to inner harmony and what they have learned
has the value of perspective.

The saints tell us, with almost one voice, of a first state
when they seemed to be two distinct persons if not the
tumult of a whole mob.   Yet they were like two persons
welded together with unbreakable chains.   Their two
selves could not live in peace, yet they could not live apart.
They were dimly conscious that the binding chain itself
was also a part of them.   It was their soul and their will,
the animating principle of their lives, torn and twisted
and stretched between the two contending selves, a state
which they called, very simply, "temptation."   From
this point, the progress of the saints might be termed the
process of making the chain into a harness, light, flexible
and sensitive, guiding the two selves into one path ahead.

It is well worth remembering, especially when about to
dip into the almost mystical sequence of O'Neill's plays,
that the saints' state of "temptation" covered the whole
gamut of evil tendencies.   There are not only ten com-
mandments (to continue the old terminology which the
saints themselves used) but seven capital sins and many
minor offspring.   Not all the saints, by any means, were
subjected to temptations peculiarly of the flesh.   Sex is
of enormous importance.   That is quite as it should be,
even from the viewpoint of a saint, when you consider
that in the act of creating new life, man is carrying on the

primary material act of creation itself. A true saint would be the last one to see any degrading implication in the idea that even mental creativeness is often impelled by the same vital instinct as sex. Nevertheless, in its narrowest sense, sex has by no means always been the chief source of temptation to the saints. Most of them have had terrific battles with pride, including its concealed form of false humility. As they have progressed on their great spiritual adventure, they have often ripped off one layer of pride only to find a dozen new layers beneath. They have even discovered themselves proud of their lack of pride !

The struggle of the saints to achieve poverty of soul has often been the hardest battle of all. Covetousness and the lust for possession may reach into a thousand inner recesses of the mind. Then there is anger — and gluttony, both spiritual and physical — and envy in a thousand forms — and sloth as a sin against the impulse of life itself. Each and every one of these the saints have recognized as sins quite as destructive to their inner natures as the more obvious sins of lust of the flesh. One of their "selves" has lived in the desire or the willingness to commit one or all of these sins. The other self has existed as a sort of ideal person, the image of the man as he would like to see himself and have others see him. Somewhere, uniting these conflicting selves, has been the innermost will and soul of the individual himself.

It is the first instinct of the poet to put this struggle of

the selves into words and, if possible, into objective characters. In the old morality plays, the authors freely
labeled their characters with the names of sins and corresponding virtues. Bunyan carried on the tradition in
English literature. The poets of our own day, like
O'Neill, are often less keenly aware of what they are
doing when they "create" characters which represent the
many "selves" of a single person. The poet, let us say,
is acutely disturbed by signs of his own potential weaknesses in people he sees about him. He suffers a sort of
agony in the presence of a proud man, but quite possibly
because he knows only too well the destructive effect of
pride to his own inner peace. He knows the imperative
need of checking his own pride and so resents furiously
the pride he sees in others. He decides to write a play
about the destructive force a proud man creates in his own
world of friends. But almost inevitably, the poet will
find another character to represent his own ideal "self,"
either as the victim or the protagonist of the proud man.
Then other characters will be added, each representing
parts of the poet's personality which pride endangers.
For he knows how devastatingly pride may reach into
every corner of his being, into his love life, into his
feminine tenderness and mercy, into his male forthright-
ness, into his spirit of friendship, even into his very creative ability as a poet. The play ends by being a complete
description of his fear of the effect of pride.

The more sensitive the poet, the more apt he is to

"project" after this fashion a great diversity of struggles between the divided selves. An ordinary mortal suffers from one or two major temptations throughout most of his life, and hardly notices his other faults. But the poet, very much like the saint, recognizes himself as beset with all the temptations in varying degrees. He lacks the smugness of the vegetable being who can say, "I am naturally honest and kind, and I have conquered most of my evil inclinations." On the contrary, the poet says to himself, "I am a strange mixture of all possible beings. Given sufficient temptation, I could be a murderer or a pervert. I could dominate nations with my pride if fate led me to be a ruler. My envy of others' talents and abilities is enough to make me lie and cheat to destroy them. I am not certain of my honesty or integrity if they were put to a real test. I am utterly weak-willed before the onslaught of my passions, and what little virtue I maintain is merely by strictly avoiding the occasions of lust. I love to possess both people and things. I am all such persons in my mind and soul and I despise myself for these hidden things which are really just as much myself as the kind, sympathetic, upright person my friends think me to be. My soul is stretched like a taut wire between all the evil I am capable of and the good I desire. I know myself for what I might so easily be, and I run cold with fear when I see this possible self in others." Sometimes the poet is incapable of putting these torturing thoughts into words. He shuns them as realities, but he

can not escape from the vague and terrifying consciousness
of their truth.

In his mind, if not in his actual daily life, the poet lives
the tragedy of the proud man or the hounding fate of the
murderer or the shame of the unnatural monster, and
whether his medium of making these inner struggles
objective be painting or sculpture or the written word or
a play, he "creates" the very thing that torments him
secretly. He projects it from his inner being to an outer
form of expression. The number of such struggles which
he gives us in his art is limited only by the possible selves
to which he is still blind.

Those who do not concern themselves overmuch with
the way of a poet often ask why he chooses this or that
"gruesome" or "morbid" subject for a novel or a painting
or a play. On meeting the poet in the flesh, they are
surprised to find that he may be a very affable and reasonable human being, "quite unlike the terrible people he
writes about." There are many good people today who
probably believe that the author of "Mourning Becomes
Electra" must show in daily life the effects of a diseased
mind. They do not understand the gulf between the
potential evil in all souls and actual wrong-doing. They
do not understand (to revert to the terminology of the
saints) the difference between temptation and sin. In
fact, they understand very little of any of the deeper
currents of life surging about them. Yet it is precisely
because the poet reacts as he does to his own potential

weaknesses that he is able to create the objective material for his work of art. Like the saints, he, above most other men, understands the sinner and fears the sin.

In the second stage of their pilgrimage, the saints tell us even more that is helpful in understanding the poet. The phenomenon of the divided self gradually gives way to a moment of apparent peace and discovery. The saint is a convert in more senses than one. He actually succeeds in converting the potential evil in his soul to a good end, recalling again the folk-lore analogy of Beauty and the Beast. He accepts the facts of his nature and through accepting them discovers that the wild beasts can be tamed. They are dangerous only so long as he fears them — and the saints have a way of seeking the end of fear through reliance on a spiritual power greater than themselves. They have called this power through the centuries Divine Grace and the source of that power God. But we are not concerned, save in passing, with the supernatural life of the saints. It is sufficient to record as a fact (though wholly inadequate as an explanation) that the saints do find a way of overcoming the fear of their own evil inclinations and of harnessing them in such a way as to draw the soul forward on its chosen road. For a time the saints find unity instead of discord. They do this and have been doing it for centuries without ever hearing of the word "sublimation." They may call their discovery sublime. But they have named the road to the discovery the exercise of the will in the love of God.

Unfortunately the saints have also discovered that the first taming of the beast is a transient victory. The beast has many forms. The saint may have tamed his beast in the form of lust, only to find that the same beast has grown twice as strong in the form of untamed pride. His renewed onslaught comes with astounding violence. The saint is plunged again in darkness and fear, and sometimes in that strange thing which is worse than fear, utter and devastating dryness of soul. What resistance he offers is reduced to a pure act of will unaided by emotional stimuli. In the writings of the mystics, we find this referred to as "the temporary withdrawal of Divine assistance," as if the convert were being tested as to his own strength, or were being shown once and for all his dependence on God. But, again, we are not chiefly concerned with the supernatural life. This familiar "dark night of the soul" has its counterpart and foundation in purely natural religion and in the experience of the poet as well as the saint.

One reason for assigning Eugene O'Neill an exceptionally high place among the poets of history is precisely because his poetic experiences, as objectified in his plays, correspond with such depth and intensity to the universal pattern of the mystical experience so fully described by the saints. This does not imply, even remotely, that Eugene O'Neill as a man is in the process of becoming a saint ! It merely implies that, as a poet, giving free rein to his creative imagination, he understands, partly by direct experience, of course, but even more by magnificent intuition, the universal character of the struggle between good and evil and the clearly marked stages in the pilgrimage from turmoil to peace. He, or rather, his characters have made some superb spiritual discoveries, even in his earlier plays. But the same characters, with different names, have again found themselves later on in darkness. Like the saints, they have reached a first crest, only to sink into another valley where new fears attack them and where the night is very black and without stars.

This is the universal language of the human quest, as the poets have always understood it. Odysseus found the long road home beset with greater and greater terrors as he neared his goal. The generations of the House of Atreus found no abatement in the attack of the Furies as they sought expiation for primal guilt. Dante went down into the pit of the Inferno before he found himself "pure and ready to ascend to the stars." The poetic genius of Richard Wagner, adapting folk-lore to his mystical intuitions, found ultimate release from the incest cycle of the Ring only in the death of the hero and of the gods themselves. Not until Siegfried was dead to his old self could he live again as Parsifal, the pure fool who could attain the Grail. It is easy enough to say that there is no connection between the Niebelungen Ring and Parsifal, that they were separate poetic concepts. But the unhappy Nietzsche knew otherwise. He felt the "betrayal" of the poetic concept of the Superman when Wagner brought his hero back to life as a knight of the Grail, humble before God. It was not till then that Nietzsche's adored Wagner became "human, all too human." The whole point is that Wagner did become human! He became the universal poet of human experience, instead of remaining with Nietzsche in the twilight of dead gods, fashioned in man's own image. The universal poet seeks the resurrection from the valley of the shadow of death —a release in humble surrender, or in death to the old self, from that strangely insistent pursuit "down the arches of the years."

At this point we must leave the saints, for what has happened to them after the long night of the soul is beyond the ken even of poets. Some of the saints themselves have tried to describe it, in all humility. St. Theresa of Avila has put words into the closing passages of the "Interior Castle" which almost break the reaches of the mind. But as one approaches the infinite in experience, the words and pictures of finite description fail utterly. The saints ultimately transcend universal human experience. The poet can follow them in their emergence from the long night of the soul and in their resurrection from the death to self, but he must bid them farewell when they ascend above the common experiences of this earth. He may still understand them through his profound intuition, but he is too sensitive to his own limitations and too aware of the privacy of mystical heights to wish to trespass. He remains content with understanding

; great paradox of resurrection itself and of the death-to-self which alone makes possible the new life of the soul.

In the truly great poet, then, we may expect to find a spiritual progression corresponding very closely to age-old inner struggles of the human race. This provides the inner unity to the poet's work. In the case of a playwright, we may expect to find the plots and materials of his plays widely diversified. There is no outer or objective unity between the hero of one play and the heroes of a dozen succeeding plays. Even the theme problems will vary, ranging in all likelihood through all the forms of sin and virtue. The choice of a theme problem will depend on which of the infinitely varied struggles of the two selves happens to be uppermost in his emotional life at the time he writes. The higher poetic unity between the plays will come out in the way the poet, through his objective characters, meets the successive problems.

In the case of Eugene O'Neill, it is very plain that the changing conditions of American life from the nineties to the present have largely conditioned his choice both of plot and theme. Environment has naturally made him more acutely conscious of certain inner problems than of others. The struggle of the nineties between a general smug complacency and a limited but intense idealism and devotion to beauty and art, the philosophic unrest and discontent of the succeeding decade with its intellectual pride, the defeat of scientific materialism in the great war, and the impulse to a new maturity in the disastrous years after the war — all of these national currents of mind and soul have influenced profoundly his consciousness of special forms of human struggle. But as a poet in the larger sense, he has also, in his successive handling of these problems, reflected the inner development in his own soul of the universal poet's quest. Moreover, we may well believe that his poetic progress is deeply prophetic of changes about to take place in the deeper sources of American life and emotions.

With the poet, our real concern is with the new forces of will, understanding and charity we can discover at work in the objective form of his characters. Suppose we were to say to ourselves, Robert Mayo, the Hairy Ape, and Bill Brown and Nina Leeds and Abbie Putnam and Brutus Jones and John Loving and young Richard Miller are all one person, one many-sided person trying to find a way through the maze of life's emotions, temptations, sins, victories over self, storms of false pride and moments of great peace. At first it would seem preposterous. Then, as we caught the feeling of a great poet, as we began to understand his strange inner union with the highest and lowest in human emotions, we might know in our hearts that it was not preposterous at all but the simple statement of a towering truth. We might begin to see his plays in an entirely new aspect as a progressive document of the immemorial experience of mankind. We might see about them the flickering shadow of our own day and times. We might also see something of the poet himself as an individual, living in our times, and inspired or distressed or angered by them, even limited and warped by them, but struggling constantly to rise above them to a life as broad and unlimited as the souls of men have ever known.

We would surely see something we had not seen as clearly before of good and evil in mortal conflict, of human will girding itself for the passage through the valley of tears, of the human soul crying aloud for help from a power greater than itself. Our charity might be stirred at the sight of repeated failures, and our admiration unleased at the sight of renewed struggle and increasing courage. Certainly our own problems would become clearer from this better understanding of one who is part of our own life. Eugene O'Neill is neither prophet nor saint. As his characters tell us, he has often, even as a poet, been deeply confused. Many of his darkest doubts and many of his most tragic defeats have sprung from immature emotions. But so have most of our own temptations and failures, not only as individuals but also as a nation. We should accept O'Neill as a companion on our own pilgrimage rather than as a leader, but surely as a companion whose poetic insight is deep, whose consciousness of our moral problems is vibrant, whose experience of the soul's conflict is sharper through intuition than most men's, and whose willingness to seek a path even in the darkest shadows marks an extraordinary tenacity and the quality of a high romance.

IV

"BOUND EAST FOR CARDIFF," AND THE SEA PLAYS

Fogs

ALTHOUGH Eugene O'Neill did not state a complete spiritual problem until he wrote "Beyond the Horizon" in the winter of 1918, his earlier work is exceedingly important as containing the seeds of future conflicts. This is particularly true of "Bound East for Cardiff," written in the spring of 1914, nearly three years before the rest of the *S.S. Glencairn* series. As O'Neill himself has expressed it, this play contained the germ of the spirit and of the life attitude to be found in all his more important later work.

Except for one bitter and sardonic little play of a suicide under a wife's nagging, called "Before Breakfast," O'Neill wrote nothing of importance during the years between early 1914 and the winter of 1917 when he completed the Glencairn series and a short play of a whaling captain in the northern ice called "Ile." It was in this long interval that, among other things, he studied under Professor Baker in the famous 47 Workshop at Harvard.

It is hard to determine what influence, if any, his dramatic studies had upon his later work, since, in content and feeling and technique, there is little noticeable difference between the first and the last three of the Glencairn series. "Bound East for Cardiff" is doubly important, however, from the very fact that it represented a spontaneous instinct, unharnessed by any other rules of the theatre than O'Neill's own inherited dramatic sense. As the son of a famous actor, James O'Neill, he probably absorbed more "theatre" in his growing days than most literary students of the drama would acquire in years of formal effort.

There were some still earlier O'Neill plays actually published in 1914, and written in the fall of 1913 and the winter of 1914, under the general title of "Thirst." But the most important part of this collection of five one-act plays is probably their general title, for O'Neill, above all else, is a poet who has thirsted unendingly for a solution to the gigantic problems presented by his imagination. It is this insatiable thirst which marks him as the rugged romanticist he is, forever searching and eternally restless under the conflicts of the spirit. His quest is not to be put aside for some easy and alluring opiate. He is like one driven by a mighty conscience, often groping in a black night, often stumbling through false paths, but never able to rest while the insistent inner spirit drives him on. To take his own encompassing sea as a simile, he has often been like a powerful swimmer too far from land in the stormy waters of his own poetic emotions. In fact this timeless conflict between the sea and the land runs through play after play he has written — those caught up in the arms of the sea hungering for the land, and those with their feet rooted in the soil thirsting for the far horizons of the sea. Nowhere is this conflict more clearly stated than in "Bound East for Cardiff."

The chief characters are the seamen of the British tramp steamer Glencairn — the same group that appeared later in "Moon of the Caribbees," in "The Long Voyage Home" and in "In the Zone." They include Driscoll, the Irishman, the rough and ready Yank, Smitty, the sensitive and lonely English boy seeking escape from himself, the "wizened runt," Cocky, Olson the Swede, and several others. But when "Bound East for Cardiff" was written, only Yank and Driscoll were clearly outlined. It was their problem that preoccupied O'Neill — and their problem was the universal question of death.

The scene of the play is in the seamen's forecastle on a foggy night when the steamer Glencairn is half way between New York and Cardiff. Yank is lying in his bunk, mortally injured by a fall when he was groping for a ladder and missed his footing, falling to the deck below. The ship's captain has been unable to do anything for him. Yank knows instinctively he is dying and a great fear has come over him — the fear of being alone in the forecastle with the fog whistle blowing above him and the sound of snoring men about him. It is the big blustering Driscoll

he must have with him — Driscoll with whom he has
fought time and again and made up and whom he loves
with the one overpowering human affection left to him.

The essence of the play is what goes on in the souls of
these two men as they keep the death watch together.
If, as one should in all O'Neill plays, we consider these
two men as parts of the poet's soul, the meaning of this
brief scene and its forecast of future O'Neill plays become
clear. The injured self and the strong self — above all
the self that was injured groping for a ladder, for a foot-
hold in a life of obscurity ; it is not at all difficult to see
in this the statement of a life-long struggle, repeated over
and over in a hundred varied forms. "I was just
thinkin'," says the dying Yank, "it ain't as bad as people
think — dyin' . . . I ain't never had religion ; but I know
whatever it is what comes after it can't be no worser'n this.
I don't like to leave you, Drisc, but — that's all."

Yet this same Yank, a few minutes later, recalling the
time he killed a man in self-defense, cries out "D'yuh
think He'll hold it up against me?" and when Driscoll in
some mystification at this new language asks "Who's
that ?", Yank replies, "God. They say He sees everything. He must know it was done in fair fight, in self-
defense, don't yuh think ?" Driscoll reassures him in
anything but pulpit language, and Yank becomes easier at
heart. But it is the sea, after all, that has brought him
injury, the sea that has possessed him (as it either pos-

sesses or cleanses so many other O'Neill characters) and
in death itself Yank hungers for the land — a secret he
has never dared to confess even to Driscoll, not knowing
that Driscoll himself has been hiding the same dreams.
"It must be great to stay on dry land all your life," says
Yank, "and have a farm with a house of your own with
cows and pigs and chickens, 'way in the middle of the
land where yuh'd never smell the sea or see a ship. It
must be great to have a wife, and kids to play with at
night after supper when your work was done. It must
be great to have a home of your own, Drisc... I never
told yuh this, 'cause I thought you'd laugh at me."

But then the possession of the sea sweeps over him
again, and his mind wanders in the adventures of the
sailor's life — the Argentine, Buenos Aires and La Plata,
Singapore and Sydney and Cape Town where he had
killed the man in a fight. But at the last, this tired and
injured soul breaks down again. "It's hard to ship on
this voyage I'm goin' on — alone !" he cries, grasping
Driscoll's hand. As the last sharp pain shoots through
him, he suddenly looks before him, the concealed and
rejected memory of years floating before his eyes — "A
pretty lady dressed in black." Driscoll sinks on his knees
beside the dead man, his lips moving "in some half
remembered prayer." But the poet has caught something
more than sombre tragedy in this long and lonely voyage
of the injured soul. As Driscoll is praying mutely, the

wizened Cocky comes into the forecastle. "The fog's lifted," he announces — and then stands dumbfounded as he sees Driscoll make the sign of the Cross.

In so far as the poet uses symbols, consciously or otherwise, the meaning of many later O'Neill plays does undoubtedly become vastly clearer from a careful reading of "Bound East for Cardiff." First of all, there is the poet's attitude toward death. In all lyric tragedy, which, in its very nature becomes akin to the divine comedy theme of man's ultimate end, death is more a symbol of discovery and triumph than of an end to life. There is nothing lyric nor triumphant in the suicide of a Hedda Gabler. But in such a death as Yank's there is clearly the promise, so to speak, of resurrection. "The fog's lifted!" A voyage to be made — alone. But still a voyage, without blinding fogs. A voyage of continued quest, with death — to the old self, the injured self — merely as the moment of departure. It is not even necessary to attach a religious significance to this symbolism, the whole point being that the poet does recognize the spiritual process of death-to-self which is part of every great poetic experience. Many later O'Neill plays end on this same note, just as the mystic is conscious of dying a hundred deaths in the effort to attain a higher plane of maturity and insight. But in this use of the symbolism of death as a promise of richer life, O'Neill at once sets himself apart from those who write tragedy without song and places himself among those who seek the affirmation of life even in death and so discover the song that turns all great tragedy into spiritual comedy.

Then there is the poet's statement of the problem of possession — a major theme in many of O'Neill's greatest plays. In this instance, the symbol of possession is the feminine sea. Again, as in the symbol of death, it is very important to distinguish between a fatalistic and an active use of the symbol. Time and again we find O'Neill characters possessed, at times by the sea and at other times by the land, by a dominating feminine character or by inner pride or by the grosser passions. But the possession is always clearly something surrendered to in the first instance and fought against later, at times with defeat but more often with victory. O'Neill characters are not passive victims of inevitable fates, but people with implied free wills whose state of possession is the first fruit of evil choice and sin or of weak surrender. The dying Yank admits that he has been thinking for a year of leaving the sea. "Sea-farin' is all right when you're young and don't care," he says, "but we ain't chickens no more, and somehow, I dunno, this last year has seemed rotten, and I've had a hunch I'd quit — with you, of course — and we'd save our coin, and go to Canada or Argentine or some place and git a farm, just a small one, just enough to live on." The sea has possessed Yank, and the sea has injured him — but he has been free to leave it. The possession is not beyond conquering. In later plays it is always the same, unless the possession has come about through deliberate and willful surrender or incurable weakness of spirit. The chance of release is always there for the spirit brave enough to battle for it.

The use of the land and the sea as symbolic elements conflicting for the possession of men's souls is another clear foretaste of the poet's struggle. But again, the danger to man comes from the use he makes of the land or the sea rather than from the elements themselves. Six years later, Anna Christie found the sea cleansing her soul, while her father found it the shroud of his cowardice. Four years later, Robert Mayo, in "Beyond the Horizon," found defeat in the land while his brother, Andrew, used the soil, at first, to create and found strength in it. Born in an age of triumphant materialism, when environment was proudly proclaimed as the mechanical shaper of men's destiny, O'Neill, with the intuition of the poet, was from the first a champion of the return to spiritual responsibility for the use made of environment. He was feeling, against the current of his immediate times, the larger current about to sweep over the earth in the revolution of science against materialism. Among modern writers, he was almost a voice in the wilderness crying for moral values when the world about him was smugly preaching economic determinism and the fatalism of matter.

The remaining three plays of the Glencairn series, written in the winter of 1917, have somewhat less stature than "Bound East for Cardiff," although they each reflect the conflict of contrasting natures with the all-embracing

sea. In outer form, at least, the plays are somewhat
reportorial, the language is brutal and phonographic and
one catches less of the poetic overtones than in the death-
watch of Yank and Driscoll. But in this same winter
O'Neill wrote another one-act sea play worthy of special
note, and followed it a year later with still another one
act play in which sea and land were strangely united in a
theme of greed and its ironic defeat. These plays are,
respectively, "Ile" and "The Rope."

"Ile" (Oil) is the story of a whaling captain whose
pride drives him to keep his ship in the Arctic over two
years because he will not return to meet the sneers of his
rivals without a full cargo of oil. He has unwillingly
taken his wife along on the ship, a home-loving person
with romantic ideas of the sea who is gradually losing her
mind in the vast loneliness of the icy north. But even
the sight of her failing mentality will not turn Captain
Keeney from his purpose. He puts down a mutiny and
grimly waits for the ice to break. At last his wife's frantic
appeals shake his purpose. He has just promised, for her
sake, to turn the bow of the ship south when the cry goes
up that the ice has broken. This is too much for him.
He gives loud orders to head north through the open
water as his wife loses the last shred of her sanity and,
stark mad, plays wildly and discordantly on the little
organ in the cabin. In this play there is obviously added
to the general possession theme of the short sea plays the
counter struggle of the feminine, home-loving, land-

loving self which is sacrificed to insane false pride. It is one of O'Neill's several plays of sheer defeat.

"The Rope" is a play which should be considered with "Ile" as a partial statement of the problem to emerge later and much more clearly and effectively in "Gold." It concerns the children of a miserly and scripture-quoting hypocrite who owns a farm bordering on the sea. One of his children, by a second wife, is a good-for-nothing who has stolen money from him and disappeared. The old man has placed a rope and noose in his barn on which he says this son must hang himself if he ever returns to the farm. The son does return, makes common cause with the daughter and son-in-law, and agrees to torture the old man into revealing where he has hidden some money he formerly obtained by mortgaging the farm. While the children are plotting this frantic revenge, a little grandchild plays with the rope in the barn. It breaks, and attached to the other end is the rough bag in which the gold has been hidden. The child gleefully takes the shining pieces and throws them one by one into the sea "to watch them skip."

The themes of pride leading to insanity, and the irony of gold that helps no one, both appear later in O'Neill's work, first in a defeatist one-act play, "Where the Cross is Made," and later in a full length version, "Gold," in which the poet finds a way out. What has puzzled many admirers of O'Neill's work as well as many of his severe critics has been precisely the outcropping of "morbidity" and defeat in so many of his plays, contrasted with his obviously sincere and aspiring search for forces and solutions that will draw his characters out of the mire. But if we keep steadily in mind that the inner unity of his work follows the hills and valleys of the classic poet's pilgrimage, these apparent contradictions become not only understandable but almost inevitable. It is their very quality of surge and relapse, and the increasing strength and maturity with which recurrent struggles are handled that establish the authenticity of O'Neill's poetic sweep. This does not imply for a moment that his defeatist plays are not in themselves unpleasant. They are. They are as unpleasant as the inner secrets of almost any human soul would be if we were allowed to see them, the moments of despair, of succumbing to overwhelming temptation, of failure to pierce the fogs of conflicting emotion. But ordinary mortals keep these secrets to themselves, or proudly reject them as "not being really themselves at all." Poets are apt to be franker with themselves and the world — and not always to the edification of that world. There is a real value in reticence which is very different from hypocrisy, and one can not always tell when the despairing or momentarily defeated word of a poet may have a profoundly disturbing or disrupting effect upon other sensitive souls. But that very fact makes it doubly important to treat the poet's work as a whole, to balance victories against defeats, and to trace the slow and painful process by which identical problems are met with greater and greater courage, wisdom and faith.

In the early short plays of O'Neill there is a preponderance of the defeated note, but at least in "Bound East for Cardiff" we have the early intimations of ultimate triumph, and in all of the plays we have that which is vastly important in contrast to the prevailing moods of the day in which he wrote, namely the instant recognition of evil as evil.

V

"BEYOND THE HORIZON"

Sacrifice

"BEYOND THE HORIZON" is not merely Eugene O'Neill's first full length play, and therefore important historically ; it contains more abundantly than the short plays the statement of most of the inner conflicts which appear in his later works, and thus has a present as well as a remote interest. It is the first fully rounded if somewhat vague statement of the poet's problem, like the first full notes of a recurrent theme in a great symphony, or, rather, like the first notes of several recurrent themes which later repeat themselves in clearer and clearer form and cross each other, sometimes discordantly, sometimes in harmonious cadence.

The story is a simple one objectively. James Mayo, whose farm lies near the sea, but not within sight of it, has two sons, Andrew and Robert. The invalid owner of the adjoining farm, Mrs. Atkins, has one daughter, Ruth. It is James Mayo's ambition to have his stalwart son, Andrew, a born farmer in every bone of his body, marry Ruth, and thus eventually bring the two farm properties together. But Ruth, in whom we already catch glimpses of the possessive and emotionally unstable Abbie Putnam of "Desire Under the Elms," and Nina Leeds of "Strange Interlude," is more deeply attracted by the shy and dreamy Robert Mayo. Robert was an invalid in his youth and later had one year at college. He is deeply in love with Ruth, but being too shy to let her see his love, he imagines her to be in love with Andrew. This problem of the strongly contrasting male instincts, as represented in the Mayo boys, and of the feminine instinct divided between them, as represented in Ruth, is more than the classic triangle of dramatic literature. In O'Neill's case, as he proved in later works, it is the statement in outer form of a deep and torturing condition of soul, of instincts so sharply divided that no harmonious resolution of them seems possible.

The clashing nature of the two brothers emerges in the very first scene between them, Andrew who can only belong to his environment by taking root in it, by digging his hands into the soil, by a physical expression of any and every inner feeling, and Robert, who says flatly "I'm not keen on being a student, just because you see me reading books all the time. What I want to do now is to keep on moving so that I won't take root in any one place ... it's just Beauty that's calling me, the beauty of the far off and unknown ... the joy of wandering on and on — in quest of the secret which is hidden over there, beyond the horizon." It would be easy enough to say that the brothers merely represent the familiar conflict of the "extravert" and "introvert" of psychiatric jargon, but that would be over-simplifying the problem. The real nature of the conflict seems to have more to do with subjective values and emotional instability as contrasted with objective values and emotional downrightness. An introvert might very well want to have the sense of being rooted in the soil. He might even cling so desperately to this idea as to be utterly miserable when wandering in a search over vague horizons. One might easily find an extravert with a passion for change, travel, quick variety of action and unexpected adventure. It is Robert Mayo's unstable will, which refuses to be anchored to anything for long, that makes him a pitiable figure compared to his decisive brother. Robert is the mental wanderer, always searching and never finding the port of his dreams.

The action of the play soon reveals that a large part of Robert's wanderlust is due to his unexpressed love for Ruth — and here we have the secondary theme of escape that runs throughout play after play in the O'Neill saga. Robert discovers that Ruth loves him, and not Andrew, and this is enough to reverse his decision to take a long three-year voyage with his uncle, Captain Dick Scott. But the change of heart is not spontaneous. It is not a decision of Robert's own making. It comes, in fact, from Ruth herself, who is at once fascinated by Robert's dreams and jealous of their hold over him. She has no sooner told Robert she loves him than she begins to exert her possessive and exclusive instinct. Robert must not go away on the trip now. "We'll be so happy here together where it's natural and we know things. Please tell me you won't go!" Robert wavers, but Ruth makes up his mind for him. Then he seeks to justify his change. "I think love must have been the secret — the secret that called to me from over the world's rim — the secret beyond every horizon; and when I did not come, it came to me." But when Robert wants to linger in the fields to look at their evening star rising, Ruth is more concerned about not being late for supper!

In the sense that the poet knows something of the secrets of all mankind, of the feminine as well as the masculine soul, and also in the deeper sense that he holds within him both the masculine and the feminine principle, this struggle of Ruth to dominate the imaginative and poetic Robert is of first importance to an understanding of the continuity of the O'Neill plays. If the feminine instinct in the poet's soul works with the masculine instinct all is well. But if the feminine seeks to dominate, even to suffocate the masculine instinct, then we have the seed of tragedy. We are, all of us, in a very real way, divided within. But it is not by making one inner person dominate all the others or crush the others that we win harmony and peace. It is only by letting each inner person supplement and complement the nature of the others that unity and maturity can be achieved. It is as if each person must be true to itself and renounce a possessive claim upon all the others before all can live together in a united and fruitful life.

The Ruth of "Beyond the Horizon" is not content to let Robert be himself, even his best self. She must possess his will so completely that he will be a reflection of herself rather than a separate person. The very things she loves in him, his dreams, she stands ready to crush because they give him something independent which might keep him distinct from her. Hers is the possessive love that kills the thing it loves, and time and again it is precisely this possessive feminine instinct which brings tragedy in the O'Neill plays.

The action of "Beyond the Horizon" is swift and logical from this point. It is Andrew now who seeks escape, once he has discovered that Ruth does not love him. Andrew ships with his uncle, Captain Scott. Old James Mayo dies soon after from disappointment, and the farm, left to the irresolute hands of Robert, slowly falls into decay and poverty. Robert and Ruth have a daughter who dies — a symbol, if you wish, of the ultimate futility of such a union as theirs. Ruth in the meantime discovers, or thinks she discovers, that it was really Andrew whom she loved from the first and not Robert. In a bitter rage at what is really her own destructive work, she heaps this final irony upon Robert's head just before Andrew's return from his first long voyage.

Andrew does not remain long. Something of Robert's wanderlust has now been transferred to him, but with it he has acquired the instinct to do more than till the soil. He wants to "get on," to "get in on something big" before he dies. Once having been untrue to himself in seeking escape, he has become the victim of the first stages of greed. The love of the soil has started to give way to a love of what the soil might bring him — riches. He is starting for the Argentine where he can make his fortune. The very thing that made him seek escape, his love for Ruth, has now vanished before the stronger impulse toward personal success. Hoping to set things right, he tells this to both Robert and Ruth. Ruth is left to the double bitterness of having loved twice, once to kill and once to lose.

During Andrew's absence in the Argentine, Robert, living in the prison of Ruth's hatred of him, falls a victim to tuberculosis. Tales are carried to them both of Andrew's vast success in the Argentine but both are too proud to ask for help until it is too late. Then Ruth sends word to Andrew of Robert's illness. He arrives with a specialist only to learn that Robert is dying. Robert creeps away from the house to die on the crest of a hill, looking at his beloved horizon, but Ruth and Andrew reach him in time to hear his dying words. It is now that Robert makes the discovery that might have freed all of them if they had made it sooner. Holding Andrew's hand, and commending Ruth to his care, Robert says weakly : "Ruth has suffered — remember, Andy — only through sacrifice — the secret beyond there —"

We must remember that at first the secret beyond the horizon was a vague lure to the unknown. Then it became love — the love that made Robert surrender to Ruth's possessiveness. At the end, the secret becomes sacrifice. But the discovery is Robert's and not Ruth's. There is definite spiritual illumination in Robert's death — an illumination destined to carry on through many of O'Neill's greatest plays in the male characters. But the fact that Ruth's spiritual problem remains unsolved is stated with tragic clarity in O'Neill's final stage directions. She remains silent beside Robert's body, gazing at Andrew "dully with the sad humility of exhaustion, her mind already sinking back into that spent calm beyond the further troubling of any hope." Years later, "Strange Interlude" was to end on a similar note of the ashes of exhaustion, all that was left of the possessive fires of Nina Leeds' soul.

But any discussion of "Beyond the Horizon" would be incomplete without some mention of the final conflict between the two brothers — the one episode in the play, perhaps, which links it most closely to O'Neill's consciousness of the masculine problem in American life as he then saw it (this play was written in 1918). Robert, knowing that he is dying, is facing his supposedly successful brother. He prods him with feverish questions, and at last discovers that Andrew, instead of working the soil, had been speculating in grain. It becomes Robert's turn to see clearly the spiritual turn-about that has helped to

ruin them all. "You — a farmer," he says sadly, "to
gamble in a wheat pit with scraps of paper. There's a
spiritual significance in that picture, Andy ... You're the
deepest dyed failure of the three, Andy. You've spent
eight years running away from yourself. Do you see
what I mean? You used to be a creator when you loved
the farm. You and life were in harmonious partnership
... your gambling with the thing you used to love to create
proves how far astray — So you'll be punished. You'll
have to suffer to win back —"

In this passage, we seem to have a touch of O'Neill as
the profound social poet, as well as the mirror of an
internal conflict. In a few words, he seems to be drawing
an indictment of the deep change then taking place in
American life from the creative spirit of the frontier to
the gambling greed of a more settled civilization. But
even here O'Neill does not forsake the tragic inwardness
of the problem he is stating. Andrew, too, the other
male principle of this inner battle, has killed himself by
being false. He may have started out with a more
decisive will, but he has misdirected it. He has used it
for the betrayal of the very things Robert most admired
in him. Thus each of the three main forces in the poet's
soul has met defeat in the first statement of the problem.
Robert, the subjective creative male has met death through
yielding to the possessive and dominating female, and
Andrew, in seeking to escape from both, instead of working with them as he might have done, has been untrue

even to his objective creative power. Robert sees the truth, that sacrifice would have saved them all. But he sees this too late.

One can not repeat too often that an attempt to state the poet's problem in these terms, and to trace, later, the development of this and similar problems in other plays, is in no sense an attempt to picture the problems of O'Neill the man and the individual. The poet and the man can not be entirely divorced, but they must not be confused. No greater injustice to Eugene O'Neill has been done than the attempt, so frequently made, to read autobiographical significance into his plays. As a human being, he can not but be subject to all ordinary influences of time, place and environment, but the very fact that he is a poet enables him to surpass the bounds of environment and to work among spiritual problems which are the creation of sensitive imagination and feeling rather than of living fact. If anything, the work of a great poet is apt to be prophetic of a turn which his life is about to take rather than a record of what his life has been. He sees and feels possibilities far beyond the actualities of the present. He deals with them, of course, because they have a personal interest for him. But that does not mean that he has actually lived through the experience, except in imagination. The poet is no more autobiographical in writing of deep spiritual struggles than the writer of crime fiction in detailing a fantastic and horrible murder.

This does not deny the claim of so many modern psy-

chologists that every "creative" work of art is a projection
of the subconscious personality and its struggles. There is
nothing new to this idea. The saints have been thoroughly
acquainted with it for countless centuries, and have used a
perfectly satisfactory terminology of their own to describe
it, at times a moral terminology of "occasions of sin,"
of "temptation" and of "sin" itself, and at other times
a poetic terminology, including such magnificent phrases
as the need of "dying to one's self to be born again."
The old Church theologians, for example, have always
defined serious "sin" as the combination of a "grievous
matter" (the objective nature of the act) with "sufficient
reflection" (implying the raising of the problem from
subconscious to conscious thought) and "full consent of
the will." Translating this to our present purposes, the
poet may be quite conscious of the "grievous matter" of
a certain problem, and may summon it, by reflection, from
hazy subconsciousness to an objective form, such as the
conflicting characters of a play. But he is hardly writing
autobiography in any common-sense meaning of that
word unless, at some time, he has actually given the full
consent of his own will to carrying out some phase of that
problem in his own life, in thought, word or deed.

It would be a most painful process, indeed, if, in tracing
the titanic moral struggles in many of the O'Neill plays,
we were to be afraid at every instant of trespassing upon
the private facts of Eugene O'Neill's personal life, or
upon the secret thoughts and desires he had willfully har-

bored. What he has done, as an artist of extraordinary
sensitivity, is to project struggles which his vivid imagination sees as possible realities, very much as we of lesser
gifts might ask "what would we do if we were suddenly
put in this or that circumstance ?"

The progress of the poet lies chiefly in his growing
ability to answer his self-imposed problems with increasing
maturity and spiritual insight, and in his passionate desire
to find clearer and clearer solutions to apparently hopeless conflicts. Again there is an obvious connection between the mental and emotional growth of the man and
of the poet. But the imagination of the poet may still
see as possible and beautiful a solution which the man
might be incapable of applying in his own life if faced
with a similar decision. In other words, the poet may
grow and expand faster than the man. Many a poet has
been uncharitably called a hypocrite because he has failed
to carry out in his private life the beauty of his poetic
fantasies. Wagner, the man, is scarcely to be compared
to Parsifal uncovering and holding aloft the Grail. The
reverse is true where those of extraordinarily saintly lives
have been unable to give outward artistic expression to
their lofty emotions. In studying the poetry of O'Neill
it is far better to discard entirely all thoughts of the man,
all useless comparisons and speculations, and to watch only
the course of the great spiritual pilgrimage expressed in
the poems themselves.

"Beyond the Horizon" clearly establishes a fully developed beginning of the poet's romantic quest, the spirit of search for the unseen and the unrealized, the consciousness of a sharp inner division and struggle, and the admission of a first defeat in a sense of desolation, emptiness and "spent calm beyond the further troubling of any hope." Yet in the very centre of this deathly calm glows Robert's discovery of something hitherto unsuspected beyond that dim horizon — the need of sacrifice and a hint of the creative power of suffering. Years later, in "The Great God Brown," the poet was destined to experience this glowing flame with a greater and overwhelming immediacy.

VI

"THE STRAW"

Affirmation

In many respects, "The Straw" is one of the most simply realistic plays among all of O'Neill's works until we come, thirteen years later, to "Ah, Wilderness!" Curiously enough, it is in this play that O'Neill first quotes (in parody, to be sure), the lines from the Rubaiyat which supplied the title to "Ah, Wilderness":

"A glass of milk, and thou
    Coughing beside me in the wilderness —
Ah — wilderness were Paradise enow!"

Most of the action of "The Straw" takes place in a sanatorium for the tubercular — which merits forgiveness, perhaps, for the above parody ! — but the theme, to which we must look for the progress achieved after "Beyond the Horizon," is faith and the affirmation of life.

The leading characters in the play are Eileen Carmody, the tubercular older daughter of an Irish contractor, and Stephen Murray, a newspaper reporter also a victim of

tuberculosis. They meet at a sanatorium to which Eileen
has been grudgingly sent by her father. Eileen is engaged to a young man whose family holds a position of
moderate consequence in the town, but as soon as he learns
of the nature of Eileen's illness he is far more alarmed
by the dangers of contagion than by her health.

At the sanatorium, Eileen and Murray develop a strong
comradeship, under which Eileen's health improves rap-
idly and Murray begins to take an interest in the writing
he has always wanted to do but has been too lazy or too
shiftless actually to accomplish. But as this comradeship
grows into love on Eileen's part, without any response
greater than friendship from Murray, Eileen has a serious
set-back. Murray has had some of his stories accepted by
magazines, and under the pride and stimulus of this
achievement, he begins to feel self-sufficient. At last, as
he is leaving, Eileen arranges to meet him at night outside of the sanatorium grounds and humiliates herself by
confessing her love for him.

From this moment on, her decline is rapid. Murray
writes her only occasionally from New York, and then
not at all. At last, however, the indecisive life in the city
is too much for him, and he returns to the sanatorium in
some anxiety to be examined. He finds that there is no
actual return of his disease. One of the nurses takes him
aside and tells him the truth about Eileen — that she has
so far given up hope and effort that she is doomed, and
is about to be sent away to the State Farm to die. She

urges Murray to tell Eileen a lie, to say that he loves her
and will marry her when she gets well.   Strangely stirred,
but still not recognizing his own true feelings, and how
much of his success has been due to Eileen, he goes to her
bedside and asks her to agree to marry him, and, in the
meantime, to let him send her to a small private sanatorium.

As he is acting out his part, however, the truth suddenly sweeps over him in "a passionate awakening — a
revelation."   He declares his love for Eileen with a new
and ringing sincerity, and then "suddenly his face grows
frozen with horror as he remembers the doom.   For the
first time Death confronts him face to face as a menacing
reality."   In the full tragedy of awakening too late, he
lets Eileen read her own fate in his eyes.   Then it is that
he grasps at the last straw.   He tells her that it is not
her fate but his own that horrified him.   He tells her the
saving lie that the examination showed a return of his
own disease, that he needs her as never before to save him.
Passionately, he makes one of the nurses back up his lie,
even though she tells him there is no hope.   "There are
things doctors can't value — can't know the strength of !"
he cries.   "How dare you use the word hopeless — as if it
were the last !   Come now, confess, damn it !   There's
always hope, isn't there ?   What do you *know* ?   Can
you say you *know* anything ?"   To which the nurse, on
the verge of tears, replies, "I know nothing — absolutely
nothing !   God bless you both !"

When Murray returns to Eileen's bedside, he finds her illuminated with the strength of motherly self-forgetfulness. "I'll have to look out for you, Stephen, won't I? From now on? And see that you rest so many hours a day —" As the curtain falls, she is still giving him maternal comfort in which the one light of renewed hope and faith begins to dawn for them both.

It would be hard, one feels, to overestimate the importance of this play as a key to much of O'Neill's later work. In it he abandons, to be sure, many of the larger and more striking similes and symbols found in the majority of his plays. The emotions are simpler and more direct. There is no possession by the sea or the land. It is the direct story of two human beings at grips with physical disease. O'Neill enthusiasts would probably put it down as one of his least important plays. Yet, in inner fact, it is one of the most revealing plays he ever wrote prior to "Ah, Wilderness !" disclosing above all a quality of simplicity and directness all too rare in many of his most important works, and a quality of affirmation of life and faith in strong contrast with the defeatism which has shadowed many of his moods.

"The Straw" also establishes an important interior development. It is the first full length play after "Beyond the Horizon" and carries through with singular strength the unsolved problem of Robert and Ruth Mayo. Death, as we have seen in "Bound East for Cardiff," is merely a symbol of inner change. The mere fact that a character representing a clear life principle dies in one play does not prevent that same principle from reappearing again and again in later statements of the same problem. But death as the poet uses it, almost subconsciously, is a harbinger of change. Stephen Murray, dangerously close to death, finds not only strength and life but love and the release of his thwarted abilities as a writer through a healing contact with the feminine instinct and through readiness to sacrifice himself. It would be difficult to find a more immediate development than this of the tubercular and dying Robert Mayo, student and book lover, who at last finds the secret beyond the horizon to be sacrifice. When O'Neill wrote "Beyond the Horizon," the discovery of Robert's condition came "too late." Fighting against a possessive feminine spirit, and failing to see what mutual sacrifice might have brought to Ruth and to him, Robert's case was "hopeless." But with the passing of the mood of possession, and with the acceptance of the feminine instinct as a healing thing, instead of a mortal enemy, how differently the problem presented itself to the poet! "There's always hope, isn't there? What do you *know?* Can you say you *know* anything?"

Once more we see the power of O'Neill's ultimate assertion of free will as the secret of release from possession, foreshadowed in "Bound East for Cardiff." The problem of possession has, for O'Neill, a dual aspect, the objective possessing force or idea and the subjective attitude of the person or principle possessed. More often than not, the fact of possession springs from the inner attitude of the person possessed. The Hindus have a saying that if only the inner flame is strong enough it can melt all the surrounding ice. In every-day experience we repeatedly encounter people who are "victims of circumstance" only because of a false and misleading attitude toward circumstances themselves. We also encounter men possessed by the love of power, for example, who could find instant release if they once recognized power as a means to an end rather than an end in itself. We say they are drunk with power, when what we really mean is that they have forgotten how to use power for a good end — an end outside of themselves or even as an act of sacrifice. This, in essence, is O'Neill's conception of the meaning of possession, something which kills if allowed to go on unchecked, but which (again like Beauty and the Beast) may be turned to triumphant good once the will asserts itself in the spirit of sacrifice or renunciation.

The apparent mountainous inconsistencies in O'Neill's work, the plays of defeat and destruction followed by plays of almost inspired religious search or of splendid assertion of the will to sacrifice, grow into a harmonious whole the moment we cease to regard each play as a complete statement in itself and follow instead the sequence of the plays. Like the intimate psychological connection between Wagner's Ring cycle and his Parsifal, the major theme of the poet must be read in flowing continuity, with major and minor themes, announced in one mood (or movement, if we were comparing it to a symphony) and completed in another. Just as the last lines in each play are by all odds the most important, as giving the key to the whole mood and purpose of the story, so we can not judge fairly and fully the insistency of the poet's search until we have the last lines of the last play.

In this perspective, "The Straw" is one of O'Neill's really important plays — as a temporary and partial solution, at least, of the problem of "hopeless" possession and fatal illness presented in "Beyond the Horizon." In Robert Mayo's dying words, we have the rumor of the theme of "The Straw," but no more than a rumor, like the first notes of a new melodic statement. In "The Straw" we have the larger elaboration of the new theme as it affects the subjective male instinct of Robert Mayo and the subjective feminine feeling of Ruth. In the next play, "Gold," as we shall see presently, O'Neill carries through the unsolved problem of Andrew Mayo, the objective male, but without relinquishing entirely the fresh development of Robert and Ruth achieved in "The Straw."

VII

"GOLD"

Confession

In "Gold," and in the one-act version of the same play known as "Where the Cross Is Made," O'Neill has taken almost the oldest known symbol of the possessive spirit — the metal that, strangely enough, is almost useless in itself.

The very rarity of gold means that men can not use it to satisfy deep human needs. It can not be used for pots and pans, like plentiful iron and copper. It is too soft and weak to forge into weapons or to carry structural burdens. It becomes a servant of mankind only in the arts, ranking in this sense even below clay and marble which can be used both for building and the arts. There is no more illusory value in the world than the value of gold, because what value it has comes from man himself and not from nature. Yet just because man himself has attributed a symbolic value to gold, the worship of it becomes strangely like man's worship of himself, something which stands like the Narcissus legend as the shadow of impending death.

In "Gold," the full length version of Captain Bartlett's greed, the story begins on the sands of a coral island of the Malay Archipelago where Captain Bartlett and five of his crew have been shipwrecked. Their supply of water has been practically exhausted. Only the cook and ship's boy have managed to keep a small flask to stave off the madness of thirst. The other four, Bartlett himself, Silas Horne, the boatswain, and Ben Cates and Jimmy Kanaka of the crew have begun to suffer the delusions of fever. In a sunken Malay canoe they have found an old chest filled with imitation jewelry which they have mistaken for gold —"all sorts of metal junk" as Butler, the cook, describes it, "bracelets and bands and necklaces that I guess the Malays wear. Nothing but brass and copper, and bum imitations of diamonds and things." But when Butler tries to tell Captain Bartlett the truth, it nearly costs him his life — for the Captain and his three thirsting men want to believe in their treasure. For Bartlett, his delusion means the end of all toil —"Aye, I'll rest to home 'til the day I die. Aye, woman, I be comin' home now," he says, almost in a trance, as if talking to his wife, Sarah, "Aye, Nat and Sue, your father be comin' home for the rest o' his life ! I'll give up whalin' like ye've always been askin' me, Sarah. Aye, I'll go to meetin' with ye on a Sunday like ye've always prayed I would. We'll make the damn neighbors open their eyes, curse 'em ! Carriages and silks for ye — they'll be nothin' too good — for Sue and the boy. I've been dreamin' o' this for years."

It is the poet in O'Neill that seized upon the double irony of Captain Bartlett's madness — that he should be obsessed not even by the reality of gold, itself a mere symbol, but by the symbol of a symbol, the glittering imitation hovering before the eyes of a starving man. There was a foretaste of Bartlett even in "Beyond the Horizon" in the problem of Andrew who had begun to gamble in the wheat pit with the very thing he had once loved to create. Bartlett had been a whaler, making honest money from an honest and adventurous trade. But the sight of gold makes him despise trade. "Gold! Better'n whaling, ain't she, boys?" he cries. Bartlett is distinctly a picking up of the Andrew problem, the minor problem of one play, and turning it into the major problem of a subsequent play. This, in fact, is one of the chief ways in which we can trace the inner continuity of O'Neill's work. He does not repeat the same major theme over and over with variations until it works out to a final harmonious conclusion. That would be the highly conscious method of the artisan. Instead he takes the surging impulses of life as they come, battling first with one and then with another temptation in tumultuous succession.

Thus, in "Beyond the Horizon," the problem centered around the subjective and unstable Robert seeking to live in a dream world and forced to bend to realities. There was only a hint of the reverse problem of the objective Andrew, born to meet realities but slowly yielding to the dream world of avarice. In "Gold," Captain Bartlett as the Andrew principle, becomes the center of the storm. He is a hardened man of action and realities enticed into a dream world to which he does not belong by the glitter of that which is not even real gold. In other and later plays both Robert and Andrew appear again and again, first one and then the other representing the problem which has become most acute in the poet's soul.

Captain Bartlett's aroused greed leads him to kill the two men, the cook and ship's boy, who refuse to share his delusion. A rescue ship is sighted on the horizon and the Captain and his three accomplices decide to bury their treasure with the intention of returning later. They are afraid that the cook and the boy will tell of their secret. It is actually Jimmy Kanaka, the native, who suggests killing the two recalcitrants, but Bartlett, already utterly untrue to his realistic self, allows Kanaka to go ahead. "I spoke no word, remember that," says Bartlett, trying to excuse himself, but already beginning to be haunted by the crime that was in his mind.

The rest of the play is in Captain Bartlett's home town where he builds a schooner to take himself and his three companions in guilt back to the island. In the interval, he has become white haired with the intensity of his inner struggle. He has also lost all human contacts with his wife and children. His wife, Sarah, vaguely suspects the truth, and refuses to christen the new schooner. She has heard the Captain talking in his troubled dreams. Bartlett's daughter is engaged to a young sea captain, and Nat, the son, strongly reminiscent of Robert in "Beyond the Horizon," is eager to ship on the new voyage with his father.   But Bartlett is obdurate in his determination to make the voyage alone with his three accomplices.   At last his wife, unable to stand the strain, directly accuses him of his crime.   "Confess to God and men," she beseeches him, "and make your peace and take your punishment.   Forget that gold that's cursed and the voyage you be settin' out on, and make your peace."   To which Bartlett cries "Confess and let someone steal the gold ! Ye'd make an old woman o' me, would ye, Sarah ? — an old, Sunday go-to-meetin' woman snivelin' and prayin' to God for pardon ?"   At last, to break down his wife's firm resistance, he threatens to take his son, Nat, on the voyage, unless she consents to christen the ship — the superstitious fear of sailing on an unnamed ship fighting with his determination to complete the cycle of his crime at all costs.   Mrs. Bartlett at last consents — but it is the final stroke to her failing health.   When the ship is ready to sail on the full tide the next morning, Mrs. Bartlett is dying, and while the Captain is with her, the ship sails without him.

The last act of the play contains, with important differences, the same material as O'Neill's one-act play, "Where the Cross Is Made."   Bartlett is now living with his two children, but he has fixed up a cabin on the roof of his house where, day and night, he watches for the return of his ship, the Sarah Allen. Months earlier, the ship has been reported wrecked, with all hands drowned, including young Dan Drew who had sailed with her at the last moment to prevent Nat from going. But Bartlett is now living entirely in his dream world and refuses to accept the reality. Hourly, he expects to see the Sarah Allen round the point and come into harbor with her fatal t.easure. Nothing that Nat or Sue can say will restore his reason. Not even the unexpected return of Dan Drew, who, it seems, was saved before the wreck by the attempt of the others to kill him, can convince the old Captain. By this time, his delusion has begun to affect Nat as well. The boy's greed is aroused by his father's incoherent tales until he, too, shares the belief that the Sarah Allen will return. Sue — and here O'Neill uses the feminine instinct at its best — remains the one connecting link between her father and brother and realities. The climax of the act comes when Bartlett, alone with his son, succeeds at last in so hypnotizing him with the dream of treasure that, as they look out from the cabin windows, they both see the red and green lights of the Sarah Allen, rounding the point in the moonlight. Nat rushes out into the night, just as Sue finds them together in their delirium.

In "Gold," Sue finally persuades Bartlett, by clinging desperately to his last fragmentary touch with reality, to save Nat by confessing the whole truth. Bartlett dies telling his son that he murdered the two men on the island — and that he knew in his heart that the Malay trinkets were brass and not gold at all. "That be the lie I been tellin' myself ever since," he confesses. "That cook — he said 'twas brass — But I'd been lookin' for ambergris — gold — the whole o' my life — and when we found that chest — I *had* to believe, I tell ye ! I'd been dreamin' o' it all my days ! But he said brass and junk, and told the boy — and I give the word to murder 'em both and cover 'em up with sand." As he dies, Bartlett, with his conscience finally at rest, tears in two the map of the island he has treasured all these years. But this is a very different ending from the one originally projected when O'Neill wrote his one-act version, "Where the Cross Is Made." In this version, both father and son see the ghosts of the crew of the Sarah Allen, the son takes on the father's madness, and the curtain falls as he triumphantly points to where the cross is made on the map of the island which he has just torn from his father's dead hands.

Considered strictly as a play, "Gold" falls far short, in dramatic qualities, of the theme as O'Neill must have visualized it. There is more sheer terror and ghostly madness in "Where the Cross Is Made." But considered as two contrasting poetic ideas, there are few episodes in the O'Neill saga so important as the change from nebulous despair in the short version to the final spiritual triumph of Captain Bartlett in the complete play. The short play represents a mood, the early statement of a problem without a solution. The complete play shows the poet rising above this mood to achieve release through a cleansing of the soul — a cleansing brought about through a feminine character. At the end of "Beyond the Horizon," we were left with Ruth and Andrew facing each other over the body of Robert, whose dying illumination had been the secret of sacrifice. But the future of Ruth and Andrew was still in darkness. In "Gold," Ruth, as it were, saves the spirit of Andrew, embodied in Captain Bartlett, from self destruction.

"Gold" is not a play to assume much importance in a purely dramatic examination of O'Neill's work. But it is a distinct and very important link in the chain of his poetic development, and in the sequence of the tumultuous spiritual struggles which his plays portray. Just as we find in "Beyond the Horizon" the rumor of eventual victory for the subjective aspect of the soul, so in "Gold" we find a similar rumor for the objective principle, guided by the feminine side.

VIII

"ANNA CHRISTIE"

Possession

"Anna Christie" was one of the first plays to bring
O'Neill widespread recognition.   It was completed in the
summer of 1920, a few months after "Gold."   But there
was an earlier version, written in the winter of 1919,
under the title of "Chris," and produced on "the road"
by George Tyler.   This version has never been published, so that we do not have the opportunity of comparing the progress made between two drafts, as we have in
the case of "Where the Cross is Made" and "Gold."   In
its material and background, "Anna Christie" belongs, of
course, among the sea plays.   In all else, it represents the
interweaving in one play of the two themes of possession
and release, with the sea literally giving up a reincarnation
of Yank, and the feminine spirit of Ruth, coming from
the land, where she found destruction, to seek a cleansing
in the sea.   To this is added the idea of the possessed
father, faintly hinted in the midst of the brother problem
of "Beyond the Horizon," and emerging more definitely
in "Gold."   Later, this father, reminiscent of Old Testa-

ment severity, reappears as the dominant figure in "Desire Under the Elms," in fading perspective in "Mourning Becomes Electra," and finally disappears into that finest incarnation of human fathers, Nat Miller of "Ah, Wilderness !" — a spiritual evolution of twelve years !

Judging only from the title of the first unpublished version, the father, Chris Christopherson, was at first the leading character. But in the play as we now know it, Anna Christie herself is the centre of the theme, the first feminine character to dominate completely an O'Neill play. Anna is a daughter of the sea to whom the touch of the land is fatal. Her father, once a seaman, but now the captain of a coal barge, sent her as a child to live with relatives on a farm in Minnesota. Growing up with her boy cousins in the farm isolation of the early century, she became in time the victim of their passions, fled to the city where she worked as a nurse girl, only to have further bitter experiences with the men of the family. In time she became an inmate of a house of prostitution. At last, after an illness, she writes to her father in New York, thinking him to be the janitor of a large building. In his pride, he has never dared confess to her that he has sunk as low as a coal barge. Father and daughter meet in a sailors' saloon near the waterfront. In the glow of old Chris' affection and repentance for his past sins of omission, a little of Anna's acquired hardness begins to drop away.

Chris is one of those familiar O'Neill characters who

has surrendered bitterly to the sea. He tries to explain to Anna that after her mother's death, when he was away on a voyage, he thought it was better for her never to see him. He doesn't know why he never came home to Sweden in the old days. He wanted to come home, he says, at the end of every voyage. He wanted to see Anna's mother and her two brothers — before they were drowned at sea — and Anna herself when she was a baby, but — he didn't go. He always signed up on new ships, for South America, for Australia, for China, for every port the world over many times, but never aboard a ship for Sweden. When he finally got enough money to return as a passenger, he "forgot" and spent all his money. When he thought of it again, it was too late. He doesn't know why, but that's the way with most sailors. "Dat ole davil sea make dem crazy fools with her dirty tricks. It' so."

But Anna instinctively sees the truth. "Then you think the sea's to blame for everything?" she exclaims, with a touch of scorn. "Well, you're still working on it, ain't you?"

But Chris tries to fool himself and Anna by the idea that a barge job is not really a sea job at all. "No. Ay don't gat yob on sea, Anna, if Ay die first. Ay swear dat ven your mo'der die. Ay keep my word, py yingo!"

Anna can not quite see the difference — but in spite of her growing understanding of her father's cowardice, she is deeply stirred by his real affection for her and his desire to have her stay with him. A real feeling grows up quickly between them. In his eagerness to make her stay with him, Chris unconsciously begins to paint the sea as he really feels it in his bones. "You don't know how nice it's on barge, Anna. Tug come and ve gat towed out on voyage — yust water all round, and sun, and fresh air, and good grub for make you strong, healthy gel. You see many tangs you don't see before. You gat moonlight at night, maybe ; see steamer pass ; see schooner make sail — see everytang dat's pooty." A very different story from his obsession about "old devil sea" ! Anna succumbs.

Ten days later, after a voyage up the coast, we find Chris's barge at anchor in a fog in the outer harbor of Provincetown, with Anna wholly captured by the mystery and romance of the sea. "I love this fog !" she exclaims to her father, who is trying to make her go to bed. "Honest ! It's so — funny and still. I feel as if I was — out of things altogether." But Chris is again in a mood of hate for the sea. "Fog's vorst one of her dirty tricks, py yingo !" to which Anna replies with a laugh, "Beefing about the sea again ? I'm getting so's I love it, the little I've seen," and later, "I don't wonder you always been a sailor." When he protests vehemently, as if with a premonition that he is losing her to the sea, she cries out "It makes me feel clean — out here — 's if I'd taken a bath."

One sees here the beginning of O'Neill's passionate

theme of "belonging" which was to reach its climax shortly after in "The Hairy Ape." Both Chris and Anna belong to the sea and can not escape from it. "I feel old," Anna explains, "like I'd been living a long, long time — out here in the fog. I don't know how to tell you just what I mean. It's like I'd come home after a long visit away some place. It all seems like I'd been here before lots of time — on boats — in this same fog... And I seem to have forgot — everything that's happened — like it didn't matter no more. . . And I feel happy for once — yes, honest ! — happier than I ever been anywhere before." To which Chris replies with foreboding, "Ay tank Ay'm damn fool for bring you on voyage, Anna." They both belong, but Chris in abject slavery and fear, and Anna in the deep joy of her native element, one belonging in chains, the other in freedom of the spirit.

It is at this moment that the sea plays its ironic prank on old Chris, throwing up at the edge of the barge a boat load of starved seamen from the wreck of a steamer — and among them the Irish stoker, Mat Burke. In the end, it is Mat who claims Anna for his own, thus completing the cycle that Chris had feared, that she, like all of her family before her, would be claimed by Ole Davil Sea. Burke is a big, sprawling and boastful man of the sea, a cross between Driscoll and Yank, of "Bound East for Cardiff." He mistakes Anna at first for a woman of the waterfront, but is deeply contrite when he discovers she is really Chris' daughter. "I'm a hard, rough man," he explains, "and I'm not fit, I'm thinking, to be kissing the shoe-soles of a fine, dacent girl the like of yourself. 'Tis only the ignorance of your kind made me see you wrong. So you'll forgive me, for the love of God, and let us be friends from this out." Burke, too, knows the enthralling hardship of the sea, but when Anna asks why he doesn't leave it he can only cry out, "Work on land, is it? Digging spuds in the muck from dawn to dark I suppose? I wasn't made for it, Miss." He, too, belongs.

Burke is not slow in telling Anna that he wants to marry her. "I'm telling you there's the will of God in it," he says, "that brought me safe through the storm and fog to the wan spot in the world where you was!" But old Chris, overhearing this, and aghast at the thought of losing his daughter to the sea can only shake his fist into the foggy night in bitter rage and shout "Dat's your dirty trick, damn ole davil, you! But, py God, you don't do dat! Not while Ay'm living! No, py God, you don't!" The sea holds the will of God for Burke, who knows its hardships without fear; but the sea becomes the will of the devil for Chris, who yields to its dominion in fascinated fear. Nowhere has O'Neill dug deeper into the roots of evil possession than in this scene — into its subjective character and its challenge to will and faith.

"Anna Christie" is actually the story of five conflicting forces — of the destruction wrought by the land to those who belong to the sea, of the sea as a cleansing spirit to those who accept it bravely, as a she-devil of possession to those who love it inordinately and with fear, of the man and woman, each injured in a way but made for each other, and of the father who is jealous of the claim the sea has laid upon his own.   Burke loves the ideal he has made of Anna.   Anna is afraid to confess what the land has done to her.   Chris is glad of anything that will give Anna back to him.   At last, angered by the conflict about her, Anna tells both men the truth of her past life.   She sees the horror of disillusionment on Burke's face and pleads frantically with him for understanding.

"And you'd die laughing sure," she cries bitterly, "if I said that meeting you that funny way that night in the fog, and afterwards seeing that you was straight goods stuck on me, had got me to thinking for the first time, and I sized you up as a different kind of a man — a sea man as different from the ones on land as water is from mud — and that was why I got stuck on you, too.   I wanted to marry you and fool you, but I couldn't.   Don't you see how I've changed?   I couldn't marry you with you believing a lie — and I was shamed to tell you the truth — till both of you forced my hand, and I seen you was the same as all the rest. . . Will you believe it if I tell you that loving you has made me — clean ?"

But Burke, who had promised that nothing could keep him from marrying her, who had forced the truth from her when she had told him she couldn't marry him, does not believe — at first.   For two days and nights he disappears in the dives of the waterfront.   Old Chris,

stung by the tragedy he has helped to bring about, decides
to sign up again for a long voyage — his pay to be made
over to Anna during his absence. Then Burke comes
back. In his tortured soul, he knows that Anna has been
telling the truth, that she has changed, that she loves him.
"If I was believing," he tells her, "that you'd never had
love for any other man in the world but me — I could be
forgetting the rest, maybe." But her word is not enough
— there is still the small wooden Crucifix in his pocket
which his mother had once given him, the Crucifix he had
tied around his neck on long voyages. He asks her to
swear the truth on this Crucifix — which she does, only
to have Burke remember, in a last agony of doubt, that
she is a Lutheran after all ! But then he looks into her
eyes, and what he sees sets him at rest. "If your oath
is no proper oath at all, I'll have to be taking your naked
word for it and have you anyway, I'm thinking," he says
slowly, "I'm needing you that bad !"

In this triumph of faith, Anna and Burke are again
united. Even old Chris, finding that he and Burke have
signed up on the same ship together, is almost reconciled.
But his premonitions will not leave him. As a rumor of
more fogs to come in the poet's weary journey, beyond
the light of the moment, we find old Chris at the end
still looking out into the night. "Fog, fog, fog, all bloody
time. You can't see where you vas going, no. Only dat
ole davil, sea — she knows !"

It is not hard to see, in this play, the mood of regression

creeping upon the poet's soul after the simple affirmation and hope of "The Straw." There is only a partial sense of defeat in "Anna Christie," to be sure — the defeat of the father who can not shake off his fearsome bond to the sea. Anna and Burke, belonging but "unpossessed," can look bravely ahead. But even they feel a vague hint of uneasiness. There is a little of bravado as they drink "to the sea, no matter what!" It is perhaps worth remembering that three years earlier, even before the first draft of Anna Christie was begun, O'Neill had written a story (never published) in which was the germ idea of "The Hairy Ape" — the play in which the forebodings of Anna Christie were to blaze again into full terror, ending in the embrace of the Beast. In the meantime, the immediate effect of the approaching regressive mood was to show itself in a new type of conflict, apparently far removed from the seductions of either sea or land, in that first play of titanic pride, "The Emperor Jones."

IX

"THE EMPEROR JONES" AND "DIFF'RENT"

Pride and Frustration

THE upshootings of pride command a large emphasis in
O'Neill's intuition of the soul's pilgrimage. In this, as
in few other aspects of his work, he speaks with the force
of universal spiritual experience. Conflicts of the flesh
can be overcome through discipline, through avoidance or
through an understanding which permits sublimation.
But pride lurks around every corner — pride that other
temptations have actually been conquered, pride in one's
own virtue, pride in one's apparent humility, intellectual
pride, the moral pride of the Pharisee, pride in positive
achievement, pride in the form of sheer obstinacy, or pride
in sudden release from bondage. It is seldom recognized
until it has closed in upon the soul. It comes without
warning and in many disguises and often after refreshing
moments of true illumination. In essence, it leads to self-
sufficiency and at last to self-worship, withdrawing the soul
from its sense of dependence upon a higher spiritual force.

Pride in one or more of its multitudinous forms enters
into nearly every O'Neill play, but in certain plays, no-

tably "The Emperor Jones," and "Lazarus Laughed," it becomes the dominating theme. It seems to follow, almost invariably, a growing mood of regression, as if it were a heartbreaking attempt to exalt a lower and despised self toward which the soul had been sinking. In "The Emperor Jones," the use of a negro as the leading character clearly indicates the nature of the spiritual struggle, especially when Brutus Jones, in his fevered fantasies, recedes, with atavistic directness, to days of slavery and bondage in the galleys. It is not a question of superiority or inferiority of race, but of the historical symbol which the negro has become through centuries of bondage.

Dramatically, "The Emperor Jones" is one of O'Neill's most important early plays. Through bold and novel technique, it created a mood in the theatre never before felt, the beat of the tom-toms, starting at the rate of the human pulse beat and rising bit by bit as a fevered pulse would rise, blending with the visual images created in the jungle by a fevered brain to express an emotional climax of rare intensity. But the intensity of the spiritual struggle is even greater. The story is of a Pullman porter who was arrested for killing another negro in a "crap" game, who broke jail by killing the white foreman of a chain gang, and escaped as a stowaway to a small island of the East Indies where, applying the tricks of the white man, he soon made himself "Emperor" of the superstitious natives. He is not, as one might suspect, a seeker for power and glory. "You didn't s'pose I was holdin' down dis Emperor job for the glory in it, did you?" he scornfully asks Smithers, the local Cockney trader and crook, with whose assistance he has worked out his schemes of robbing the natives.   "Sho!   De fuss and glory part of it, dat's only to turn de heads o' de low-flung, bush niggers dat's here.   Dey wants de big circus show for deir money.   I gives it to 'em an' I gits de money."

Then, laughing at his own contempt for his own laws, he asks : "Ain't I de Emperor ?   De laws don't go for him.   You heah what I tells you, Smithers.   Dere's little stealin' like you does, and dere's big stealin' like I does. For de little stealin' dey gets you in jail soon or late. For de big stealin' dey makes you Emperor and puts you in de Hall o' Fame when you croaks.   If dey's one thing I learns in ten years on de Pullman ca's listenin' to de white quality talk, it's dat same fact.   And when I gits a chance to use it I winds up Emperor in two years."

This passage sets the whole problem of Brutus Jones in clear relief.   His is not the obvious pride of the power seeker or of mere vanity, but the pride of lower instincts, long held in bondage, seeking to copy the worst faults of the higher instincts under which he has lived in terror and subserviency.   He is like an enslaved mankind to whom Prometheus has suddenly brought the use of fire. His first instinct is to despise all those who are still in bondage, to turn traitor to his own and to enslave them, as he has been enslaved, by superior knowledge and trickery.

He is, if you want, symbolic of all those who suddenly find themselves freed from old chains, and use their freedom to despise and destroy others, of all the snobs and new-rich of the world who grow fatuous on the continued miseries of those they have left behind.

The play opens at a moment when the natives have at last been pushed beyond endurance and are planning the "Emperor's" overthrow. A stroke of luck has helped Jones in his dizzy climb — the misfire of a bullet directed at his breast. He seized upon this incident to make the natives believe he had a charmed life and that none but a silver bullet could kill him — again, if you wish, the symbol of that superstition by which the dishonest rich have made the world believe that their very riches could save them from the revenge of their victims, and that only one of their own sphere of iniquity could meet them on equal grounds. But the silver bullet has another and individual meaning for Jones. It is white. It is superior. It is the symbol of the white man's mask under which he works. It is the symbol of his pride of release from bondage, the fetish of his particular pride. On this he places his reliance when he sees that the "Emperor game" is up. He has no regrets at abandoning the trappings of power. His plans are all made. He will escape to Martinique, where his stolen money is safe in a foreign bank, and the natives will never catch him so long as he is protected by the legend of the silver bullet.

Jones goes forth alone toward the forest, with the

vengeful tom-toms of the natives beginning to beat in his
ears.   But he fails to find the food he has hidden at the
edge of the forest.   He must now plunge alone and
hungry through the jungle.   The beat of the tom-toms
grows more insistent, more rapid.   Shadows of fear begin
to creep upon him.   He shoots them — using the first of
his six bullets, the last of which is a silver bullet, with
which he will kill himself rather than be killed by the
natives.   As he plunges deeper and deeper into the jungle
morass, the ghosts of his old sins rise before his fevered
eyes — the colored man he had killed, playing dice in
rhythm with the beat of the tom-toms ; the foreman of
the chain gang, his other victim ; then, as a racial throw-
back, the slave auction and finally the galleys.   Four
more bullets to explode the four visions.   And with each
bullet, a more and more rapid beat of the tom-toms.
Stripped almost naked, exhausted and mad with fever,
Jones suddenly begins to pray to the God he has defied, a
prayer of terrified supplication.   But the beat of the tom-
toms only grows louder, more urgent, faster.   Jones, in
terror, uses his last bullet.   At last the natives close in
upon him.   They shoot him — with silver bullets they
have made by melting down silver coins !

"Emperor Jones" marks the first of the more imaginative O'Neill plays, in which direct symbolism and fantasy
begin to take the place of more realistic characters who are
only indirectly symbolic.   But it is obviously the mode of
expression rather than its content that begins to change.

The seeds of "Emperor Jones" can be found in every play that preceded it — in the state of bondage to the sea or the land, in the lust for gold, in Andrew Mayo's gambling with what he once created, in the disease burdened characters of "The Straw," in the downtrodden water-front characters of "Anna Christie"— in all the oppressed and sinning and struggling humanity that the poet instinctively used to illustrate the terrors, true and false, of souls in slavery or dejection.   In their partial illuminations are the seeds of the very pride of release which brings the downfall of Brutus Jones, the pride of premature discovery and unmastered, undisciplined freedom.

"The Emperor Jones" is a play of profound disillusionment, but not of total blindness.   The poet knows that pride must die before there can be a true release.   There is something of the purge of true tragedy to the play. But in the killing of Jones with a silver bullet, there is a rumor of pride still unconquered.   As the malicious Smithers leans over the negro's corpse, he exclaims : "Silver bullets ! . . . Yer died in the 'eighth o' style, any-'ow !"   In the poetic, rather than the literal and dramatic sense, there is a concession here to pride itself which foreshadows further onslaughts.   There is not even true dramatic irony in this trifling incident, of the kind to be found in "The Rope."   Brutus Jones would have been proud to know that he had been killed with silver bullets — a final triumph for his quick wit and superiority !

One striking difference between this and earlier O'Neill plays is the almost total absence of the feminine quality. The only female character in the play, an old native woman, sneaks out of the Emperor's abandoned mansion in the very first scene — leaving the battle against pride to be fought out as a purely masculine task. In a broad way, this association of pride with the male principle, as contrasted with possessiveness in the female principle, runs through all the O'Neill plays. Again this seems to be another evidence of the poet's instinctive use of a universal language. In all folklore, the abstraction of pride has been easier to symbolize through men than women, through gods rather than goddesses. The concrete, protective, maternal instincts find natural expression in the feminine symbols, in the sea, the mother earth or in the character of a woman. Woman is the nemesis of pride, as of all abstract sins. It is no mere chance, therefore, but something inherent in a struggle of pure pride, that the woman in "Emperor Jones" is the last to leave before naked pride is left to find its own destruction.

The reappearance of the feminine idea, however, in O'Neill's next play, also written in the fall of 1920, is not very comforting. "Diff'rent" is, at first glance, one of the most distressing and complex of O'Neill's works — the story of a woman so tenacious and inhuman in her idealism that she brings destruction to herself and the man she loves. It is really a study of the distortion that comes to the feminine soul when it abandons concrete instinct and tries to live in the rarefied atmosphere of an abstract ideal, in other words, when it is not true to its own nature.

In a setting of "scrupulous neatness" and rigid order in a seaport village of New England, Emma, the daughter of Captain John Crosby, rejects the hand of young Captain Caleb Williams, to whom she has long been engaged, when she discovers that he is not "diff'rent" from all other sea-faring men, including her own father. As a matter of fact, he is vastly different from most of them, his only offence against the moral code in many long years of whaling trips being on one occasion when his crew, cynically amused at his indifference to women, persuaded a native girl to swim out to his ship when they knew she would find him alone. Even on this occasion, he tried manfully to resist the combined temptation of the native beauty, the seductive climate and the sense of "being away from everything." But the story of this one misadventure, told as a huge joke by the other seafaring men of the town, gets back to Emma's ears, and is enough to close the book of her life to Caleb. Caleb remains the same, but her ideal of him, and of their marriage as something "diff'rent," has been shattered. Even her mother's appeals are of no avail. "It'd be jest like goin' agen an act of Nature for you not to marry him," her mother pleads, "Ever since you was children you have been livin' side by side, goin' round together, and neither you nor him ever did seem to care for no one else...

You'd ought to remember all he's been to you and forget this one little wrong he's done." But Emma is obdurate — not because she could not readily forgive the same mistake in other men but because "it makes him another person — not Caleb, but someone just like all the others."

Here we have, of course, a resurgence of the feminine possessive claim. Emma must possess what no others of her acquaintance have, a concrete case of an ideal. Her lips are ready enough to forgive, but not her heart. She can not have faith in the future if her ideal of the past has been broken. "I ain't got any hard feelings against you, Caleb — not now," she explains to the bewildered and contrite young Captain. "It ain't plain jealousy — what I feel. It ain't even that I think you've done nothing terrible wrong. I think I can understand — how it happened — and make allowances. I know that most any man would do the same, and I guess all of 'em I ever met has done it... I guess I've always had the idea that you was — diff'rent... And you was diff'rent, too ! And that was why I loved you. And now you've proved you ain't. And so how can I love you any more ? I don't, Caleb, and that's all there is to it. You've busted something way down inside me — and I can't love you no more."

But her possessive instinct will not let him alone. When he starts to go, she holds him back. She doesn't want him to leave her "with no hard feelings." She, herself, will never marry — but she wants Caleb to remain her friend. Before he leaves, she has brought him to a point where he tells her that he will never marry anyone else, that he will wait for her to change her mind, "thirty years if it's needful." Emma, herself, is possessed by her abstract ideal, but she in turn possesses the soul of Caleb — a shriveled echo of the possessive Ruth Mayo of "Beyond the Horizon" in whom the concrete and the ideal were also at war, wanting all so much that she obtained nothing.

The second act of "Diff'rent" is thirty years later — the allotted time that Caleb would wait "if it's needful." During all these years, Caleb has never failed to call on Emma when his ship was in port. But in the last two years, something new has come into her shriveled life — a dissolute nephew of Caleb's, back from the war, and still in the army. On this boy Emma showers all the affection her befuddled nature can command, giving him money for his gay parties and liquor. Obviously somewhat out of her head, she has even tried to dress again as a young girl. When, in a moment of fear that he will be disinherited by his own family, he offers to marry her, Emma accepts — and then breaks the revolting news to Caleb. Caleb kills himself, and, a few minutes later, Emma, having discovered too late that the boy had merely been making fun of her, follows Caleb's choice.

It would be difficult to find a redeeming feature in this play of negation and madness. So far as it reflects the poet's intuition of a soul in distress, it is a moment of utter despair, the male instinct throttled, the feminine denying its own instincts, a complete deadlock of emotion, of aspirations and ideals, ending in utter defeat.   The play is even stiff and ungainly in its technical handling, as if expressing even in outer form the momentary sterility of the poet's soul.   There is a complete lack of subtlety and distinction in the statement of the first act conflict, the unforgiving rigidity of Emma being contrasted with a too ready condoning of faults by others instead of with a spirit of forgiveness that at the same time recognizes the real nature of the guilt.   There is none of that deep compassion combined with indignation so often found in O'Neill's work, by which he can "love the sinner and hate the sin."   It is as if the death struggle of pride in "Emperor Jones," with the desertion of all feminine aid, had left the poet's will and perceptions almost paralysed and a ready victim to bitterness and a black night of the soul.   At this moment, the regression from the first heights of "The Straw" is complete — the first nadir of the poet's cycle of quest.

X

"THE FIRST MAN"

Partial Acceptance

THE "death" of the creative spirit is always a tragic moment for the true poet — children lost before they have known manhood and womanhood. In "Diff'rent," O'Neill, the poet, must have experienced as never before the strangulation of the creative impulse, the feminine part of the soul at deadly war with the masculine, resulting in utter spiritual sterility and the raising of the symbol of death in its aspect of defeat. But such an impasse can not last for long when the will of the poet is stronger than the emotional knot binding him. It is wholly characteristic of O'Neill's driving determination to find a way out that, in his next play, the battle should be against the memory of death and end in a renewed though partial acceptance of the creative demand upon life. That, in essence, is the theme of "The First Man," written only a few months after the completion of "Diff'rent."

The leading characters in "The First Man" are Curtis Jayson, an anthropologist, and his devoted wife, Martha, who has been his companion on many far journeys in the quest for old bones. The other characters, mostly Curtis' smug brothers and sisters and family connections, represent chiefly the composite of intolerant and suspicious public opinion, alert to smell evil and consecrated to preserving appearances. Richard Bigelow, an old friend of Curtis', acts as the sympathetic interpreter of the real Curtis. In the early part of the play, we learn that Curtis is at heart and always will be a romanticist, that his passion for searching the dead past began only after the death of his first two children. In the delusion that they were somehow preserving the sacred memory of those children, Curtis and Martha resolved never to have children again, to lose themselves in their joint work. Curtis is even now about to set out on a five year expedition to find the remains of the "first man" in the central Asian plateau north of the Himalayas, and has obtained special permission to bring Martha with him.

In terms of poetic impulse, this opening theme is the perfect sequel to the period of regression which began with the fogs of "Anna Christie" and continued with acceleration through "Emperor Jones" and "Diff'rent." The great affirmation of life and hope in "The Straw" gave way slowly to creative doubt and then to despair — the death of the children who have become only a memory and an obsession to Curtis Jayson. Overshadowing fear of again assuming the creative burden has turned him to the dead and forgotten past, even to the very first concept of man. If the creative future is filled with fogs and doubts and darkness and struggles, it is easier and less fearsome to "lose one's self" in the past and among the dead. But life still makes demands, and in "The First Man" the will of the poet has found the expression of this demand in the woman, in the very symbol that denied life in "Diff'rent." For Martha, as yet unknown to Curtis, is to satisfy her deep inner craving and have another child. Thus we have once more the recurrent O'Neill attitude toward the feminine idea, the power that can suffocate or cure, destroy or create.

When Martha finally tells Curtis what is to happen, we have an immediate sharpening up of the poet's real conflict. Curtis' world is "blown to bits"; they can not go on "living the old, free life together"; the appearance of a new life will separate them, make them no longer sufficient unto each other. But Martha pleads with him for understanding — "I've felt myself feeling as if I wasn't complete." There is an imperative work of her own to be done which is not part of his purely masculine work. "If you had just the tiniest bit of feminine in you!" she exclaims. "But you're so utterly masculine! ... I love the things you love — your work — because it's a part of you. And that's what I want you to do — to reciprocate — to love the creator in me — to desire that I, too, should complete myself with the thing nearest my heart!" But Curtis will not listen. He can not understand. For a moment he even urges her to destroy the life that has begun, until he sees the utter horror in her eyes. This scene between the lost masculine soul and the feminine soul re-discovering itself is perhaps one of the most directly revealing statements in all of O'Neill's plays. This time it is the man who has turned possessive in his sterility. "You are me and I am you!" he cries, as if Martha could not possibly have a life outside the orbit of his masculine way of escape. But Martha whispers to him, "Yes, you love me. But who am I? You don't know." The curtain descends on this life and death struggle, with Martha and Curtis "held by each other's fearfully questioning eyes."

But it is Martha, the creator, who wins out. Curtis postpones his joining of the expedition until the time for the child's birth. Then the law of birth — pain — delivers its mightiest blow at Curtis. During the months of waiting, Curtis has not been able to rid himself of his fear of new life. He has actually hoped that the child might be born dead — so that his old life with Martha might be renewed. But it is not the child who dies. It is Martha. She lives just long enough to ask Curtis' forgiveness — when he knows in his heart, and for the first time, that it is he who must be forgiven. The swift tragedy staggers him, gives him a moment of insight, but does not conquer him completely. "She loved me again — only me — I saw it in her eyes!" he cries out with an almost diabolic triumph. "She had forgotten — *it*. It has murdered her! I hate it — I will never see it — never — never — I take my oath!" And with this vow in his heart, he rushes back blindly to the dead Martha.

But the poet was determined, this time, to carry through the battle for Curtis' salvation. Where Martha's own pleadings had failed, where her death had failed, and where, in a mood such as that of "Diff'rent" all else might have failed, the final battering down of Curtis comes through the irony of public opinion as summed up in the evil suspicions of his own family. Understanding nothing of the real struggle between Martha and Curtis, they have become convinced that his hatred for the child is due to the fact that the child is not his own. In their hearts, and openly when Curtis was not present, they have been accusing Bigelow of being the real father. They feel the finger of disgrace upon the family name, and when Curtis is about to leave without seeing his child, they finally tell him their suspicions, begging him "officially" to recognize the child for the sake of the family good name. In his disgust and horror at this attack on both Martha and the child, Curtis at last finds his true manhood. He will give them "the only answer." He goes to the child's room, and returns with "a look of strange exultation on his face." He looks from one to another of the accusers. "Well — my answer to you — your rotten world —" he exclaims, "I kissed him — he's mine ! He looked at me — it was as if Martha looked at me — through his eyes." Then he leaves the child in the care of his old aunt, Mrs. Davidson, who had herself been childless, the "one Jayson with unmuddled integrity to whom I can appeal." Of her he makes this request, "keep him with you — out there in the country — never let him know this obscene little world" (indicating his group of relatives). "Teach him his mother was the most beautiful soul that ever lived."

It is again characteristic of the poet's soul in turmoil that Curtis Jayson's victory over himself should not be complete. He does, in a measure, complete his manhood through the strange paradox of adding just "that tiniest bit of feminine" for which Martha had yearned. It is feminine intuition that makes him understand the look and the meaning in the eyes of his child. By that very intuition he becomes more of a man. Yet his work in the dead past still remains paramount. The forming of the child's mind is to be left to another — to a frail and ageing woman. He, himself, still seeks escape from the responsibility of creation, that dread thing which had twice caused him unbearable pain.

In one sense, "The First Man" makes it plain that the O'Neill drama — the continuous drama running through all the plays — centers vibrantly around the problem of the creative deadlock. Nothing can bring more acute pain and distress to the creative poet than the forces which make creation impossible, which set up a barrier between the feminine and the masculine and prevent their harmonious union. Yet we see time after time that the engulfing forces objectified in the O'Neill plays are nothing more nor less than destructive agents of that union so passionately desired by the poet. The overwhelming sea, the fog, the alluring horizon, the possessive gold, the pride springing from inferiority — all of these are hateful barriers to be shattered or scaled before the elements of the soul can be at peace with each other. Sacrifice, hope and affirmation of life, and acceptance of pain as the law of birth — these are some of the weapons by which the poet strives to break through to creative unity. Yet none of them brings permanent relief from the conflict, because, intermingled with them are the disturbing remnants of fear and pride, the elements of spiritual immaturity which carry with them the seeds of renewed disaster. It is one of the most astounding yet logical coincidences in the O'Neill saga that the only partial victory of "The First Man" with the hero still looking backward along the path of human existence should bring forth, in immediate sequence, that first great tragedy of deep regression and introversion, "The Hairy Ape."

"The First Man" was completed in the winter of 1921. "The Hairy Ape" was completed in the fall of the same year as the culmination of an idea that had been growing in the poet's mind since 1917. But in tracing the amazing sequence between these two plays, it is also well to remember that the idea for "The Fountain" was also taking shape during the summer of 1921, the germ of a new quest born in the very death pains of an old one — again the emergence of a new symphonic theme beneath the notes of a dying climax.

XI

"THE HAIRY APE"

Escape

No ONE has understood better than Eugene O'Neill that
the soul at war with itself belongs nowhere in this world
of realities. The soul that denies or seeks to escape from
its own creative power sinks in misery below the beast.
In "The First Man" we have a conventional statement
of the theme, clear and articulate. In "The Hairy Ape"
we have a restatement of the theme in the rough and
inarticulate regions of the soul, ending in death through
the embrace of the beast.

Curtis Jayson, in "The First Man," after rediscovering
part of his manhood, found himself still bound by the
passion of his search for the dead origins of his race.
He was leaving the life he had brought into being to
search for his lowly past. Carry through this idea, change
the scene to the stokehole of an ocean liner, and we have
the beginnings of "The Hairy Ape." The poet's soul
has at last found a symbol of the lowest man, in a cage of
steel. "The ceiling crushes down upon the men's heads,"
writes O'Neill. "They cannot stand upright. This ac-

centuates the natural stooping posture which shoveling coal and the resultant over-development of back and shoulder muscles have given them. The men themselves should resemble those pictures in which the appearance of Neanderthal Man is guessed at. All are hairy-chested, with long arms of tremendous power, and low, receding brows above their small, fierce, resentful eyes."

Thus, figuratively, we have Curtis Jayson at the end of his quest, back at last to the first man, but not in Asia. Instead, he has found the first man in himself — in his own soul, as it were — imprisoned in the steely symbols of today. And among the first men, he finds Yank, "more powerful, more sure of himself than the rest. They respect his superior strength — the grudging respect of fear. Then, too, he represents to them a self-expression, the very last word in what they are, their most highly developed individual." It is not hard to guess that Yank also represents a self-expression of the distracted soul of the poet, utterly thwarted in "Diff'rent" and only partly victorious in "The First Man," sinking back, almost as a last resort, into his lowest human quality, brute strength, boastful in his knowledge that there is nothing lower he can reach.

The quality of introverted fantasy is plainly uppermost in O'Neill's mind throughout this play. Even his stage directions call for deliberate unreality. "The treatment of this scene," he says, "or of any other scene in the play, should by no means be naturalistic. The effect sought after is a cramped space in the bowels of a ship, imprisoned by white steel." Repeatedly, he describes the chorus of stokers' voices as having "a brazen metallic quality as if their throats were phonograph horns." The whole play is more of a subconscious dream or vision than an attempt at realistic drama. The stoke hole is Hell. O'Neill calls it that. "The Hairy Ape" is a vision of the poet's Inferno.

It is perhaps something more than a coincidence that in this play of Hell, O'Neill finds himself for the first time (though by no means the last, since "Dynamo" was still to be written) under the mental and emotional cloud of late nineteenth century science, and the spiritual chaos it produced. He finds himself running directly counter to the universal spirit of human folk-lore, which resolutely regards human nature as something needing redemption after a fall, a return to primal inner peace and perfection. It was nineteenth century science that immediately assumed a primitive man emerging from the beast as a necessary corollary to the doctrine of evolution, that assumed (and then rationalized the assumption) the evolution of a soul as well as a physical organism, and thereby twisted the idea of a redemption into the idea of a gradual ascension. The instinct of the race spoke otherwise, not alone in the Biblical concept (which, as we have seen, Saint Augustine found quite compatible with his ideas of evolution) but in all such persistent folk-lore as the fables of Prometheus or of Pandora. Our scientists

of today, having been shocked out of their nineteenth century smugness by new atomic theories and the death of
materialism, are more cautious in their assumptions.   A
few antique minds still persist in the old strain, the scientific untouchables ; but the first enthusiasm over a possible
Simian ancestry has given way to a spirit of cautious
inquiry and an examination of other equally possible and
plausible theories.   Even the idea of spontaneous generation of new species at certain "ripe" stages of the earth's
development is receiving honest consideration again.   But
the fact remains that when O'Neill wrote "The Hairy
Ape," science had given the psychological idea of possible
regression an enormous impetus.   The worldly concept
had changed from redemption—in which man could
safely look backward to discover a gleam of hope for the
future—to evolution, in which man could look backward
only in fear and horror.

One of the most interesting passages in the first scene
of "The Hairy Ape" is when O'Neill, speaking first
through Yank and then through the ancient Irishman,
Paddy, shows his instinctive cleavage to the older idea
which impatient science was attempting to destroy.   Yank
has been boasting that the men in the stokehole are better
than "the baggage" in the first cabin.   "Who makes dis
old tub run ?   Ain't it us guys ?   Well, den, we belong,
don't we ?   We belong and dey don't.   Dat's all."   But
the old Irishman who has been listening half drunkenly
to this boasting, this pride in being at the bottom, suddenly

"cries out in a voice full of old sorrow." As the men stare at him, startled, he says : "We belong to this, you're saying? We make the ship to go, you're saying? Yerra then, that Almighty God have pity on us! Oh, to be back in the fine days of my youth, ochone! Oh, there was fine beautiful ships them days — clippers wid tall masts touching the sky — fine strong men in them — men that was sons of the sea as if 'twas the mother that bore them. Oh, the clean skins of them, and the clear eyes, the straight backs and full chests of them!" Then, in one of the most luminous passages O'Neill has ever written, Paddy goes on to describe the sight and sound and smell of the sea and ships. "'Twas them days a ship was part of the sea, and a man was part of a ship, and the sea joined all together and made it one." Then, scornfully, "Is it one wid this you'd be, Yank — black smoke from the funnels smudging the sea, smudging the decks — the bloody engines pounding and throbbing and shaking — wid divil a sight of sun or a breath of clean air ... feeding our lives along wid the coal, I'm thinking — caged in by steel from a sight of the sky like bloody apes in the Zoo!"

But Yank will have none of the dream of the past. "Hell in de stokehole? Sure! It takes a man to work in hell. Hell, sure, dat's my fav'rite climate. I eat it up! I git fat on it! It's me makes it hot! It's me makes it roar! It's me makes it move! Sure, on'y for me everything stops. It all goes dead, get me? ... I'm at de bottom, get me? Dere ain't nothin' foither. I'm de end! I'm de start!...Slaves, hell! We run de whole woiks. All de rich guys dat tink dey're somep'n, dey ain't nothin'! Dey don't belong. But us guys, we're in de move, we're at de bottom, de whole ting is us!" There is both splendor and terror in Yank's pride in being at the bottom, in his scorn for past days that were cleaner and better and freer. Paddy is the O'Neill calling for redemption from a fallen state. Yank is the O'Neill blazing with pride in belonging to the low past, and seeking to glorify the lowest state into the highest — pride in going back to the ape, Curtis Jayson, transformed, passionately seeking the first man of an age that no longer saw man in God's image and as a creator under God's law.

But a feminine character again destroys this masculine complacency — an anaemic feminine character, to be sure, but none the less feminine. Mildred Douglas, the granddaughter of a steel puddler who became a steel master, is one of the first class passengers. In her weary and disillusionised way, she wants to know how the "other half" lives, has dabbled somewhat in social service, and has an abstract sympathy for the poor and an understanding of the snobbery of her own kind. She visits the stokehole of the ship and comes upon Yank at a moment when he is railing against the tyranny of the ship's officers who are driving the men to feed the blazing furnaces. She is filled with horror and terror at the sight of him and at the sound of his rage. She cries to the engineers, "Take

me away! Oh, the filthy beast!"—and faints. This
is the blow that upsets Yank's complacent pride and makes
him "try to tink." The others accuse him of falling in
love. "Love, hell!" he cries. "Hate, dat's what.
I've fallen in hate, get me?"

But love it is—and hate, too. For the first time, Yank
sees himself as the hairy ape, the lowest form of life
aspiring to something higher to which he can never "belong." His pride in being at the bottom, in being "the
works" of the thing of steel, has been shattered, and by a
woman. When the boat reaches port, Yank's search for
revenge begins. To Fifth Avenue he goes, in front of a
Church, hoping to find the object of his love and hate.
But the people he sees do not see him. They are masked
automatons. When he calls them names, they do not
hear. When he throws himself against them in his rage,
it is he who recoils, not they. They merely answer "with
mechanical affected politeness" and say "I beg your pardon." Yank is arrested and thrown into jail.

In jail Yank hears for the first time of the I.W.W.—
hears from a politician's speech in the newspapers that they
believe in blowing up the world with dynamite. His rage
now turns to the passion for destruction. "Steel! It
don't belong, dat's what! Cages, cells, locks, bolts, bars
—dat's what it means!—holdin' me down wit him (the
steelmaster) at de top! But I'll drive trou! Fire, dat
melts it! I'll be fire—under de heap—fire dat never
goes out—hot as hell—breakin' out in de night—"

But when he does get out of jail and tries to join a local of the I.W.W., he again finds that he does not "belong." The I.W.W., hearing his violent intentions, think he is an agent provocateur and throw him out bodily. The last shred of his contact with the world has been broken. He belongs nowhere. When a policeman finds him sitting disconsolately on the sidewalk, "tryin' to tink," and asks him what he has been doing, Yank replies: "Enuf to gimme life for ! I was born, see ? Sure, dat's de charge. Write it in de blotter. I was born, get me !"

The last scene of the play is one of O'Neill's most memorable strokes of fantasy, when the bewildered Yank finds himself face to face with a gorilla in the Zoo. Yank talks aloud to the gorilla, who seems to understand him. "I s'pose yuh wanter know what I'm doin' here, huh ?" he asks. "I been warmin' a bench down to de Battery — ever since last night. Sure. I seen de sun come up. Dat was pretty, too — all red and pink and green. I was lookin' at de skyscrapers — steel — and all de ships comin' in, sailin' out, all over de oith — and dey was steel, too. De sun was warm, dey wasn't no clouds, and dere was a breeze blowin'. Sure, it was great stuff. I got it aw right — what Paddy said about dat bein' de right dope — on'y I couldn't get *in* it, see? I couldn't belong in dat. It was over my head. And I kept tinkin' — and den I beat it up here to see what youse was like."

This whole passage becomes a terrifying picture of a soul that has slipped its anchor to the world. Yank even

feels that the ape is happier than he — a deep and rich
recognition that man, even if he would, can not find himself by going back to the beast. "It's dis way, what I'm
drivin' at," Yank tells the Gorilla, "Youse can sit and
dope dream in de past, green woods, de jungle and de rest
of it. Den yuh belong and dey don't. Den yuh kin
laugh at 'em, see? Yuh're de champ of de woild. But
me — I ain't got no past to tink in, nor nothin' dat's
comin', on'y what's now — and dat don't belong. Sure,
you're de best off! Yuh can't tink, can yuh? Yuh can't
talk neider. But I kin make a bluff at talkin' and tinkin
— a'most get away wit it — a'most! — and dat's where de
joker comes in. I ain't on oith and I ain't in heaven, get
me? I'm in de middle tryin' to separate 'em, takin' all
de woist punches from bot' of 'em."

Here we have, in the crude language of Yank, the most
profound problem of the disjointed and divided soul, rebelling not only at the burden of creating, as in "The First
Man," but at the very possession of intellect itself, at the
very distinction between man and beast, at the burden of
thought itself and the tragedy of being born a man. Man
searching for peace in mere animal instinct and finding
that even then he can not throw off his manhood. The
answer? Escape even from thought. "A little action,
dat's our meat!" he cries at the gorilla, "Dat belongs!
Knock 'em down and keep bustin' 'em till dey croaks yuh
wit a gat — wit steel! Sure!" In a sudden access of
furious exaltation, he breaks open the gorilla's cage to set

him free—but then mocks at him with a last touch of proud superiority. The gorilla wraps his arms around Yank and crushes him to death. In his last feeble moment of life, Yank crawls into the gorilla's cage to die. "And, perhaps," concludes O'Neill, "the Hairy Ape at last belongs."

Taken by itself, "The Hairy Ape" is a play of sheer terror of life covered with a mask of mocking pride. But like all other O'Neill plays, it can not be taken alone. It catches the raw horror of a mood, and gives vent to that horror with a brutality almost unparalleled in dramatic literature. But even in its worst moments, it never wholly loses sight of things outside. There is always the vision of the Irishman, Paddy, and Yank's strange understanding that, in spite of everything, he is not a beast, that his racial consciousness can not go back to the unthinking quiet of the jungle. When he does, even mockingly, seek comradeship with the beast, it brings death—another of those mystical deaths to an old self in which the O'Neill fantasy abounds. Moreover, there is the strange insistent sequence of the regression from the soaring faith and hope in life of "The Straw." Reaching at last its lowest elements, the creative burden is the price paid for intellect and thought. Then why thought—and why life itself? "I was born, get me?" The indictment against life itself! If the inner struggle of the poet's soul ended there, we could put it down as utter defeat. But "The Hairy Ape" was not to be the end. The renewed aspiration of "The Fountain" was already gathering strength in the poet's crushed soul. "The Hairy Ape" was to be only a symbol of the dark despair that sometimes sweeps over the soul to disappear later in a triumph of sheer will.

XII

"THE FOUNTAIN"

Tenderness

"Why have I lived ! To die alone like a beast in the wilderness ?" When O'Neill, speaking through the mouth of the wounded Juan Ponce de Leon, asks this question, we catch the faint and almost unrecognizable echo in "The Fountain" of the death of the Hairy Ape. But in the answer to his own question, we find the new vision of hope breaking into the very darkness of earlier despair. Neither the poet nor the mystic can ride from crest to crest of discovery and understanding. There is always a valley between to be traversed. The mere fact that many poets have kept these dark and bewildering moments to themselves and have let us see only their clearer visions does not alter the universal nature of the experience. O'Neill has bared the poet's soul at every stage of the painful journey. But that makes him different from many hundreds of poets only in his willingness to let others know the entire range of the conflict. It does not make the conflict itself nor its stages differ in the least from the most profound experiences of the human race — an insatiable driving quest for inner unity and peace, to be found by the saints in God, and by others in varying degrees either in God or in whatever it may be that they acknowledge to be greater than themselves and outside of themselves. For O'Neill, the ultimate quest has always been God.

"The Fountain," the immediate vehicle of O'Neill's recovery from the depths of "The Hairy Ape," is not among his successful plays. In form it is somewhat long and rambling, in content more philosophical than dramatic, and in some of its closing scenes, which are highly visionary, it presents scenic difficulties of a kind to obscure the poetic intent. But as part of a spiritual sequence it is very important. What, for example, could be more revealing of inner continuity than the very first description of Ponce de Leon as "a romantic dreamer governed by the ambitious thinker in him." It was the very act of thinking at all which the Hairy Ape sought to escape. Yet out of his death rises the ambitious thinker, one whose thoughts govern even his dreams. The jungle has been left behind. The poet is again looking ahead, eager to meet life once more on its own terms.

In the early scenes of the play, Juan meets a woman who has loved him too well — Maria. It is thus that Maria describes Juan as she bids him farewell : "You are noble, the soul of courage, a man of men. You will go far, soldier of iron — and dreamer. God pity you if these two selves should ever clash ! You shall have all

my prayers for your success — but I shall add, Dear
Savior, let him know tenderness to recompense him when
his hard youth dies !"　Here we have, in a new challenge to life, the old conflict of the two male selves —
and again it is the prayer of a woman that they be united
in the intuition of tenderness.　So much for the first
statement of the problem.　The second part of the theme
— the rumor of the new quest — comes in a song sung
to Juan by Luis de Alvaredo :

> Love is a flower
> Forever blooming.
> Life is a fountain
> Forever leaping
> Upward to catch the golden sunlight,
> Striving to reach the azure heaven ;
> Falling, falling,
> Ever returning
> To kiss the earth that the flower may live.

But Juan, the ambitious thinker and hard adventurer,
will have none of this.　"The devil seize your flower !"
he mocks.　"Do fountains flow only to nourish flowers
that bloom a day and die ?"

Yet, when the Spanish nobles persuade an old Moor
to tell them of the mysteries of the fabulous East, it is
Juan who listens to his tale of "a sacred grove where all
things live in the old harmony they knew before man

came. Beauty resides there and is articulate. Each sound is music, and every sight a vision. The trees bear golden fruit. And in the center of the grove, there is a fountain — beautiful beyond human dreams, in whose rainbows all of life is mirrored. In that fountain's waters, young maidens play and sing and tend it everlastingly for very joy in being one with it. This is the Fountain of Youth . . . The wise men of that far-off land have known it many ages. They make it their last pilgrimage when sick with years and weary of their lives. Here they drink, and the years drop from them like a worn-out robe." Already the seed of Maria's prophecy is taking root — the conflict of the dreamer and the soldier of iron.

Soon after this, Juan is disgraced at court as the result of a duel, and accompanies Columbus on his second voyage "to Cathay." Several Spanish nobles are with him, among them the dissipated Luis de Alvaredo, who had first sung him the song of the fountain. Juan is still the soldier and adventurer, unable to understand the almost religious exaltation of Columbus. Then, twenty years later, we again find Juan as the resident governor of Porto Rico. But now his hair and beard are gray. "His expression and attitude are full of great weariness. His eyes stare straight before him blankly in a disillusioned dream. The lines about his compressed lips are bitter." Luis de Alvaredo is still with him, but has now become a Dominican monk and has achieved "a calm, peaceful expression as if he were at last in harmony with himself."

It is Luis, now, who seeks to bring wisdom to the ageing Juan. "You must renounce in order to possess." But Juan will still have none of this. "The world would be stale indeed if that were true!" he exclaims irritably. His dreams are still of the mythical Cathay, and, more than ever, of the fountain of youth. Twenty years of small duties have not blunted his dream. He is even now seeking a patent from the King of Spain to continue on to Cathay.

An Indian, Nano, is brought before Juan—and Nano again fires the dream of Cathay and youth with legends of the tribes from which he sprang. And then comes another impulse to the passion for renewed youth in the person of Beatriz de Cordova — the child of that Maria whom Juan had once loved, of Maria who, still lonely and childless, had foreseen the conflicts of his soul when she bade him farewell and returned to her husband. In her renunciation of Juan, she had at last found, in the coming of Beatriz, the answer to her prayers. To Juan, Beatriz becomes the reincarnation of his youth and romance, all that Maria might have been to him had she been free and had he then been capable of love. Beatriz has been made Juan's ward, and brings him his commission to explore the land of his dreams. And with it, she brings him the last message from Maria. "I recall something she said I must remember when we should meet," says Beatriz. "'Bring him tenderness,' she said, 'That will repay the debt I owe him for saving me for you.' She said these

words were secrets to tell you alone.   What did she mean,
Don Juan?"   But Juan does not answer her directly.
"Tenderness?" he muses.   "Do you bring me that,
Beatriz?   No, do not — for it means weakness.   Bring
me the past instead.   Give me back — the man your
mother knew."

In the ensuing scenes, the drama of Juan's soul is
worked out in the symbols of Beatriz, his lost and now
desired youth, of Nano, the figure of the myths for which
Juan is ready to sell his soul, and the greed of the
Spaniards who want Juan to lead them to Cathay and
gold.   Nano, as Juan believes, holds the key to the secret
of the east — the fountain of youth.   But Nano, although
imprisoned and put to torture, persists in saying that
"only the gods know" where the fountain can be found.
Juan will not leave for Cathay without the secret, although
the populace, eager to begin the hunt for gold, believe
that Nano has bewitched him, and demand the Indian's
death.   At last Nano, asking the forgiveness of his tribal
gods, tells Juan the lie that he does know where to find
the fountain and will pilot his ship for him.   The rebellion of the people is put down and Juan, torn between his
love for Beatriz and the need of rediscovering his youth
in order to gain her love, sets sail for the mythical islands.

Nano leads the Spaniards to the Florida coast, where
he secretly rejoins his old tribe and plots with them for
the death of Juan.   They are to lead Juan to a spring,
to tell him that this is the fountain of youth, and while

he is gazing into its depths, kill him. They carry out
their plan, and just as Juan, who has prayed to Beatriz
and the spirit of youth and drunk of the waters, discovers that he has been betrayed, the Indians let fly their
arrows and leave him for dead. But he has only been
wounded. He awakes in the gloom of the forest to cry
to the Son of God for justice and magnanimity. "True,"
he cries, "I prayed for a miracle which was not Thine.
Let me be damned then, but let me believe in Thy King-
dom! Show me Thy miracle—a sign—a word—a
second's vision of what I am that I should have lived and
died! A test, Lord God of Hosts!" He speaks half
in bravado, half in supplication. But the vision does
come to him—of forms rising in the great fountain that
plays about him in his delirium—the form of Beatriz,
then the form of an old Chinese poet, of the Moorish
minstrel, and through all the song of the Fountain.
Then, again, other characters, with the symbols of their
religions carried before them. Juan murmurs: "All
faiths—they vanish—are one and equal—within...
What are you, Fountain?—That from which all life
springs and to which it must return—God? Are all
dreams of you but the one dream? I do not know.
Come back, Youth. Tell me this secret!"

Then the vision of an old Indian hag suddenly melts
into the form of Beatriz and Juan cries: "Beatriz! Age
—Youth—They are the same rhythm of eternal life"—
and later he prays: "O God, Fountain of Eternity, Thou

art the All in One, the One in All—the Eternal Becoming which is Beauty!" He falls unconscious, the
vision disappears and the dawn comes as Luis, who has
escaped the vengeance of Nano and the savages, comes to
rescue him.

The last scene of the play returns to the realistic mood,
with Juan waiting for death in a Dominican monastery in
Cuba. It is now his nephew, another Juan, who has come
from Spain to claim and win the heart of Beatriz—the
youth of God's constant creation. Juan understands at
last and gives the young couple his blessing. When they
have gone, Juan dies in the arms of Luis, crying out in
ecstasy, "Oh, Luis, I begin to know eternal youth! I
have found my Fountain! O Fountain of Eternity, take
back this drop, my soul!"

There is much pathetic and groping uncertainty in "The
Fountain" in spite of the poet's evident feeling of exaltation and discovery. Perhaps the key to this uncertainty
may be found in the very conflict stated at the outset—
the romantic dreamer governed by the ambitious thinker.
The poetry of O'Neill is never at its best when it becomes
highly conscious and rationalized, when the "ambitious
thinker" is dominant, and throughout "The Fountain"
there is the pale cast of intellectual effort seeking to guide
the more spontaneous search of emotion and intuition.
It is a perfectly natural reaction from the struggle against
thought itself in "The Hairy Ape," but it is not a wholly
triumphant or successful reaction. Among other things,

there is not a complete escape from the pride of "The Hairy Ape." Just as Yank took pride in the thought that he belonged at the bottom, so Juan ultimately finds an exalted pride in the pantheistic vision that he is part of God —a drop in that Fountain of Eternity which is the great Becoming and the great Beauty. The leap from the pit of hell in "The Hairy Ape" to the sense of being part of God in "The Fountain" is too sudden. It partakes too much of the pride of sudden release found in "The Emperor Jones."

The pantheistic concept, after all, is merely another subtle form of anthropomorphism, an attempt to create God in the image and likeness of man and of that nature of which man is a part. It is as if the sphere were to liken itself to the center of the sphere. The center of the sphere, after all, has no dimensions. It has no finite extension, no right nor left. Just as a man at the north polar axis of the earth could look in only one direction— south— so, at the center, there would be neither north nor south nor east nor west. Space and time, measurable dimensions, in other words, are symbols of the finite. The center, which cannot be measured, which has no dimension and therefore no possibility of error, is, in a sense a symbol of the infinite. Rhythm, movement, the principle of Becoming, are all attributes of the sphere, but not of the center. Thus the pantheistic concept, which would identify the infinite with the attributes of the finite, denies all of our experience of the distinction between the sphere and the center. It is an attempt to place finite limitations upon the infinite—and this, again, is the essence of anthropomorphism, a form of exalted self-worship. "The Hairy Ape," rebelling against the burden of thought, sought identification with the lowest forms of nature; Ponce de Leon, relying on ambitious thought, seeks identification with the highest and most beautiful in nature. The difference is really in degree only, and in the symbols selected. There is no difference in the sense of a true release from finite bonds and a complete renunciation of self-worship.

Even a misguided quest, however, reflects the essential courage of the poet. If perfection and full illumination were attainable at once, there would be no such thing as a mystical pilgrimage of the soul. There would be no divided selves to bring into harmony, no bitter internal conflicts to resolve in maturity, no evidences, as the saints would have seen it, of the effects of an original sin from which the soul must be redeemed. "The Fountain" does express the nobility of persistent ecstatic search, even if it leaves us with the feeling of a false discovery and of premature exaltation. It also gives us the natural prelude to the theme of O'Neill's next play, "Welded," in which the agonies resulting from self-worship are carried forward in the objective terms of a man and a woman, united yet at war—the sphere, so to speak, seeking an impossible unity in its own finite differences, rather than seeking harmony through the center.

XIII

"WELDED"

Divided Self

"The Fountain" was written in the fall of 1922. "Welded" was written the following winter. What manner of man is it that succeeds to the mantle of Juan Ponce de Leon — the romantic dreamer dominated by the ambitious thinker? O'Neill's description of Michael Cape, the husband in "Welded," is as follows: "His unusual face is a harrowed battlefield of super-sensitiveness, the features at war with one another — the forehead of a thinker, the eyes of a dreamer, the nose and mouth of a sensualist. One feels a powerful imagination tinged with somber sadness — a driving force which can be sympathetic and cruel at the same time. There is something tortured about him — a passionate tension, a self-protecting, arrogant defiance of life and his own weakness, a deep need for love as a faith in which to relax." Had the poet deliberately intended to do so, he could not have written a clearer description of the self-worshipper, seeking completion of himself in the symbol of himself — of Juan

seeking peace in identification with his Fountain and finding only the torture of incompleteness.

The description of the woman — the successor of the
Beatriz symbol — is more objective and superficial. But
her face, we read, "lacks harmony. It is dominated by
passionate, blue-gray eyes, restrained by a high forehead.
. . The first impression of her whole personality is one of
charm, partly innate, partly imposed by years of self-
discipline." There is little of Beatriz here, of the woman
carrying the gift of tenderness, and much more of the
projection of Michael's own desire for completion — passionate eyes in contrast to his own dreamer's eyes, a placid
high forehead as against his own forehead of a thinker,
charm and discipline against his own passionate tension
and self-protecting defiance. Throughout the play, two
circles of light "like auras of egoism, emphasize and
intensify Eleanor and Michael." Thus, at the very outset, we have the inevitable result of self-worship — discord, tension and irreconcilable differences — the East and
West of the periphery of the sphere.

Michael is a playwright, Eleanor an actress. Both are
successful in their fields. But in the very intensity of
their love for each other they find torture which years of
married life have only intensified. The play starts with
Michael's return from a self-imposed exile during which
he has been completing his last play. They greet each
other with the ardor of lovers, but in every word they

find the seed of renewed conflict. The very intensity of their desire to live within and become the other destroys the freedom of their love — for Eleanor is always seeking herself in Michael and Michael is seeking himself in Eleanor. Recalling the first days of their marriage, Eleanor exclaims, "I lost myself. I began living in you. I wanted to die and become you!" And Michael insists that "Our marriage must be a consummation demanding and combining the best in each of us! Hard, difficult, guarded from the commonplace, kept sacred as the outward form of our inner harmony!" But Eleanor instinctively feels some of the danger of this passion for self-realization. "Sometimes I think we've demanded too much," she says sadly, "Now there's nothing left but that something which can't give itself. And I blame you for this — because I can neither take more nor give more — and you blame me! And then we fight!" And then the whole pride of Michael bursts forth in this rejoinder : "Then let's be proud of our fight! It began with the splitting of a cell a hundred million years ago into you and me, leaving an eternal yearning to become one life again."

Here, as clearly as the poet can put it, we have the yearning of Ponce de Leon to become one with his Fountain — the anthropomorphic desire to find peace where there can be no peace and unity where there can be none — a complete self in the periphery where there can be only divided selves.

The action of the play is comparatively stilted, and in no sense measures up to the intensity of the theme. A few minutes after Michael's return, the solitude of their love is interrupted by a knock at the door, which Michael wishes to ignore. But Eleanor, after a brief struggle with herself, insists on answering it. She can not accept the complete absorption in themselves which is Michael's measure of perfect love. The intruder turns out to be her theatrical manager — a man for whom Michael feels a furious but groundless jealousy. His visit is brief, but it serves to stir the devil in Michael. There follows a scene in which Michael and Eleanor torture every old wound — each speaking more to self than to the other. But their words are even more revealing than those of the first scene of the true nature of their fatal attraction to each other.

"I feel a cruel presence in you paralyzing me . . . grasping at some last inmost thing which makes me me — my soul — demanding to have that, too ! I have to rebel with all my strength — seize any pretext ! Just now at the foot of the stairs — the knock on the door was — liberation !" This passage from Eleanor is followed by many others in the same vein, and by Michael's countering charges, such as : "I've grown inward into our life. But you keep trying to escape as if it were a prison. You feel the need of what is outside. I'm not enough for you. . . At every turn you feel your individuality invaded — while at the same time, you're jealous of any separateness in me. You demand more and more while you give less and less. And I have to acquiesce. Have to ? Yes, because I can't live without you ! You realize that ! You take advantage of it while you despise me for my helplessness !"

At length Eleanor, feeling the burden of his possessiveness intolerable, tells him the lie that she was formerly and is still the mistress of John, her producer. But Michael is too proud to think that she could possibly love another. He sees her action only as revenge. "You did this out of hatred for me !" he cries. "You dragged our ideal in the gutter — with delight ! And you pride yourself you've killed it. . . But I tell you only a creator can really destroy ! And I will ! I will ! I won't give your hatred the satisfaction of seeing our love live on in me — to torture me ! I'll drag it lower than you ! . . . I'll murder it — and be free !"

In the next two scenes, both Michael and Eleanor try, unsuccessfully, to "murder" the ideal of their love, Eleanor by going to John, and Michael by seeking out a shoddy woman of the streets. When Eleanor tries, miserably, to give herself to John, she is confronted by a vision of Michael, standing like an angel with flaming sword in her path, and realizes, before it is too late, that the real angel of integrity is within her. She returns to her home. Michael finds himself equally incapable of going through with his resolution. Instead, when he discovers that the prostitute gives all her earnings to her "man" and receives only a beating in exchange, he learns a lesson from her. "You got to laugh, ain't you?" says the woman. "You got to loin to like it!" "Yes!" replies Michael suddenly, "That's it! . . . That goes deeper than wisdom. To learn to love life — to accept it and be exalted — that's the one faith left to us!" He, too, goes home.

In the last scene, slowly and painfully, Michael and Eleanor work to a new understanding. Once more they try to lacerate each other, but with less power to hurt than before. Eleanor makes one more attempt to leave, but can not pass the door. "It opens inward, Michael," she says simply, and returns to him "full of some happy certitude." Then they stare into each other's eyes, and "it is as if now by a sudden flash from within they recognized themselves, shorn of all the ideas, attitudes, cheating gestures which constitute the vanity of personality. Everything, for this second, becomes simple for them — serenely unquestionable. It becomes impossible that they should ever deny life, through each other, again."

But the triumph is neither as complete nor as purging as the poet must have felt it to be when he wrote the scene, for the old desire to justify pride and self love sweep back over Michael — that pride of the fight begun when the cells separated millions of years before. "You've failed!" he exclaims triumphantly, then, "We've failed. . . We can live again! But we'll hate! . . . And we'll torture and tear, and clutch for each other's souls! — fight — fail and hate again — but! — fail *with pride* — with joy !" All the old dreams of self-realization back again — and with pride ! It is not a pleasant picture. It is a foreboding picture, capable of leading only to an access of exaggerated humility as a frantic effort at compensation.

In "Welded" we have another play with little or no rumor of creation — again the sterility of the Narcissus theme, love as the ecstasy of self-possession but not as the means to creation. All of this was implied in "The Fountain," but in both plays the seeming discoveries and their accompanying exaltation yield nothing of true humility. The pride of the Emperor Jones and of the Hairy Ape live on in Michael Cape, the thinker, dreamer, sensualist. The helplessness of the possessed still envelops the feminine instinct in Eleanor. From this stalemate, we might expect anything, but the relentless driving power of the poet's quest actually brought him to the terrible chastisement of that play of black and white miscegenation, "All God's Chillun Got Wings." In this play of profound abasement of the masculine principle, the poet was destined to find at least momentary surcease from the pride and arrogance and self-glorification of "Welded" — a valley of humility this time rather than of despair and a valley of purifying fire.

XIV

"ALL GOD'S CHILLUN GOT WINGS"

Abasement

In two important respects, "All God's Chillun Got Wings" is a direct continuation of "Welded." It is again a fruitless marriage, in which two people work to destroy each other. In that lies the outward similarity. But the inner connection is even more important. It is not unlike the sudden change from major to minor key in the same melody. "All God's Chillun" is as full of the notes of abasement and humility as "Welded" is strident with the notes and intervals of pride.

The objective story, as such, is far from universal in feeling, being the story of a marriage between a negro and a white girl. The real universality emerges only when we accept these figures as symbolic, and as a continuation of the seemingly endless effort to find an adjustment between the feminine and the masculine instincts. In the early scenes of the play we are shown black and white children playing together in the tenement districts of New York, among them little Jim Harris, a negro boy whose father was successful enough in a trucking business to leave behind him a modest fortune, sufficient to send his boy and girls to schools of higher education, and Ella Downey, nicknamed Painty-Face, because of her beautiful pink and white complexion. They are frankly fond of each other, a fact which does not seem to call for over-much comment in that neighborhood where blacks and whites "gang up" together on a basis of rough equality. Even in these early scenes, however, there is a faint and curious echo of that "will to become the other," or rather, to find one's self in the other, which was so marked in "Welded." Little Jim is talking protectingly to Ella. "You mustn't never be scared when I'm around, Painty Face," he says. But Ella protests. "Don't call me that, Jim — please !" He is at once contrite. "I didn't mean nuffin'. I didn't know you'd mind." "I do — more'n anything," replies Ella. "You oughtn't to mind," protests Jim. "Dey's jealous, dat's what." He points to her face. "Of dat. Red 'n' white. It's purty." But Ella protests again, "I hate it . . . I hate it. I wish I was black like you." And then it seems that Jim has been wishing he was white — and has been taking chalk and water, on the advice of a barber, to achieve the great result !

But nine years later, things have changed a bit. It is graduation day, and Ella, flushed with the confidence of seventeen, is running around with Mickey, a rising young prize-fighter and bully. Jim Harris is also graduating — but only on his second attempt. He is not stupid —

far from it — but his confidence disappears at examination times, with all the whites staring at him. Ella has
tried to forget their childhood friendship, but Jim is still
doggedly devoted to her, whether she cares for him or
not, and is not afraid to risk an encounter with Mickey,
the gang hero, to prove his readiness to protect the dis-
dainful Painty Face.

The special abasement, or inferiority, which O'Neill is
trying to express in this story emerges forcefully in this
second scene when Jim, discouraged by Ella's indifference,
receives some pugnacious advice from Joe, a "regular"
negro of the gang. Joe is furious at what he considers
Jim's effort to climb up from his rightful place. "Listen
to me, nigger," he shouts, "I got a heap to whisper in yo'
ear! Who is you, anyhow? Who does you think you
is? Don't yo' old man and mine work on de docks togidder befo' yo' old man gits his own truckin' business?
Yo' ol' man swallers his nickels, my ol' man buys him
beer wid dem and swallers dat — dat's the on'y diff'rence.
Don't you 'n' me drag up togidder?" Jim dully tries to
protest that he is Joe's friend still. But Joe will have
none of this implied superiority. "No, you isn't!" he
protests. "I ain't no fren o' yourn! I don't even know
who you is! What's all dis schoolin' you doin'?
What's all dis dressin' up and graduatin' an' sayin' you
gwine study be a lawyer? What's all dis fakin' an' pre-
tendin' and swellin' out grand an' talkin' soft and per-
lite? . . . Tell me befo I wrecks yo' face in! Is you a

nigger or isn't you ?   Is you a nigger, Nigger ?   Nigger,
is you a nigger ?"   Then Jim looks quietly into Joe's eyes,
and says simply, "Yes.   I'm a nigger.   We're both niggers."

The effect of this short statement is miraculous.   All
Joe's rage wilts at once.   He offers Jim a cigarette and
lights it for him.   Then, with vast satisfaction, as if the
whole world were now understandable, he asks : "Man,
why didn't you 'splain dat in de fust place ?"

In all of O'Neill's writing, there are few scenes as utterly revealing of the true nature of one of the poet's
major problems — the difficulty of facing the reality of
one's own soul and of accepting it.   Time after time, the
O'Neill characters struggle to be something other than
they are, to wear the outer mask of this or that personality, to live up to this or that pose, only to meet tragic
defeat because they will not accept the truth.   In the very
earliest statement of the problem, Ruth, in "Beyond the
Horizon," would not accept Robert Mayo for what he
was, and sought, through possessing him, to make him
something different.   Captain Bartlett, in "Gold,"
thought the precious metal would alter his whole life, and
remove him from the despised sphere of "trading."   Old
Chris, in "Anna Christie," would not face his own weaknesses, and blamed them all upon the possessive "davil
sea."   Brutus Jones sought to play the white man in his
empire of cheating and evil.   And then, with sudden
clarity, in "Diff'rent," the whole problem found first

place. Emma could not accept Caleb as he was —
though he was far better at that than most of the men she
knew, including her own father — but must have him
something else, something "diff'rent" or not at all.   Above
all, and supremely, so far as poetic expression goes, in
"The Hairy Ape," pride would not let Yank accept himself for what he was.   He must exalt his job "at the
bottom" into the superior task of life.   He must, to satisfy his own mind, consider himself "de woiks."   And
because he would not accept himself, his mediocrity or
his lowliness, if you will, he could not belong anywhere.
Even the gorilla would not have him.   He found himself
— "perhaps" — only in death.   Ponce de Leon would not
accept his advancing age as part of the life principle, and
finally sought a false substitute for resignation in identifying himself with his pantheistic god of the Fountain.
Neither Michael nor Eleanor in "Welded" would accept
themselves as the individuals they were.   They sought
something more — the becoming of the other person as
well, as a means to self-worship of a false self.   And
then, in the sudden and simple admission of one negro
boy to another that "We're both niggers," the whole
fabric of pretence disappears like a foul mist.   The masks
are discarded for the realities.   Joe no longer resents even
Jim's education.   His last words in the scene are a friendly
reminder — "Time you was graduatin', ain't it ?"

But the problems of the soul — and certainly of the
disturbed soul of a poet — do not settle themselves in one

flash of fine intuition. "All God's Chillun" continues to carry through the tragedy of the humble black soul, wishing it were white, and of the proud white soul, wishing first that it were black, too, and then dreading, beyond all else, that the black soul might really become white and equal. Ella Downey, after another five-year interval, finds herself discarded by Mickey, the prize-fighter. Her child by him has died — again that recurrent theme of the death of the child of pride first heard in "Beyond the Horizon." She is now ready, in her weariness, to accept the protection offered by the patient and essentially humble Jim. They are married, but not before we again find Jim, with ambitions rearoused, hoping against hope to pass his law examinations in spite of the panic that always overtakes him, and Ella, ready to take Jim for just what he is, and secretly dreading the very success he hopes for. By marrying him, she temporarily triumphs — for he wants to take her abroad to live where people will not notice the difference in their race. He does not ask for her love, only to be able to be near her, to keep harm away from her — "to give my life and my blood and all the strength that's in me to give you peace and joy — to become your slave ! — yes, be your slave — your black slave that adores you as sacred !"

Two years more pass — and Jim has to bring Ella back. They were happy for a brief spell in other lands, where people were kind to them, but then Ella's liking for Jim changed to love. They became man and wife in

reality as well as in name, and this acceptance of reality
and its danger of creation of new life — life that would
be humble and black — began to unsettle Ella's mind.
Jim brings her back to the house which his mother has
decided to give him as a wedding present, a house dominated by a portrait of Jim's father and by a large black
Congo mask which his sister had given him.   Jim is
again determined to go through with his law studies — in
the pathetic belief that Ella will at last be proud of him
as a member of the bar, and that his willingness to fight
out their fate will give him new strength in her eyes.   He
feels that in going abroad, they were both seeking a
cowardly escape.

But Ella, now half crazed, and giving freer vent to
the fight between two inner selves, wants to have Jim only
as a child again — in the innocence and freedom from
creative obligation of the days when they were just little
Jim Crow and Painty-Face.   She does not want him to
pass his examinations.   The Congo mask sums up for her
all the objects of her dread and hate.   It is that Thing
which she will not accept — a lower self striving toward
equality.   She wants the negro only as the little slave boy
— the playmate — or in the image of the harmless "Uncle
Jim" with whom she lived for a year abroad before liking
turned to love — and hate.   Trying to cope with his insane wife and his studies is too much for Jim.   He fails
again — but in his failure, Ella finds joy, and a return
to a childish peace of mind.   She ceases utterly to be a

woman, but with womanhood pass also her fear and rage,
and her desire to kill.

"Everything'll be all right now," she chatters on, with
the harmless insanity of a child. "I'll just be your little
girl, Jim—and you'll be my little boy . . . and I'll put
shoe blacking on my face and pretend I'm black and you
can put chalk on your face and pretend you're white just
as we used to do—and we can play marbles—only you
mustn't all the time be a boy. Sometimes you must be
my old kind Uncle Jim who's been with us for years and
years. Will you, Jim? . . . And you'll never, never,
never, never leave me, Jim? . . . 'Cause you're all I've
got in the world—and I love you, Jim." But the kiss
she gives his hand is the tender and grateful kiss of a
child.

In his utter self-abasement and resignation before this
tragedy, which he finally accepts, Jim at last receives illumination. "Forgive me, God, for blaspheming You!"
he cries. "Let this fire of burning suffering purify me of
selfishness and make me worthy of the child You send
me for the woman You take away!" And, as Ella tugs
at his hand and begs him to come and play with her, he
cries out again, "Honey, Honey, I'll play right up to the
gates of Heaven with you!"

There are many reasons for believing that this play
marked one of the major crises in O'Neill's life as a poet
of the soul in torment. After all, what the play itself
represents in the course of the poet's pilgrimage is clear

enough — at least a temporary humbling of the male instinct, accompanied by a spirit of resignation, and an acceptance of the creative or feminine instinct as being still
that of a child.   It is the child in all of us that fears
the possessive monsters of our own egotistical selves.   It
is immaturity which makes us cry for the moon and refuse
to be content with moonlight.   And by contrast, the first
real step toward maturity is apt to be the sudden and complete acceptance of one's actual immaturity — a sudden
smashing of the false image of ourselves we have been
eager to worship and the discovery, in its place, of a
very weak and humbled reality which we must live with
but can no longer worship, which we must work with
under a force greater than ourselves in humility, suffering
and purification.   Nothing could be more essentially immature and childish than the mood of exalted pride in
self-torture in which "Welded" ends.   It is like the final
outburst of a punished child crying "Beat me, beat me —
go on, beat me!"   Yet, in the case of a fundamentally
strong character, determined, in spite of every transient
mood and fog, to find a way out, such a flowering of pride
could only lead to a great crisis in which real self-respect,
based upon true self-appraisal, would be discovered for the
first time.

That the conception and writing of "All God's Chillun" amounted to just such a crisis of self-revelation (and
revaluation) is simply borne out by the very different
character of all of O'Neill's subsequent works.   The ele-

ment of struggle does not cease by any means at this point. But the essential character of the many complex struggles changes abruptly.　They become less and less the conflicts of realistic and egotistical individuals, and take on more of the hue and magnitude of great forces of good and evil at work in the soul.　The play characters are still individuals, of course.　But their passions have greater dimensions and in a very special sense greater dignity, as if they reflected the tales of mythology rather than the fables of the nursery.　Even in his earliest plays, of course, O'Neill's intellectual attitude gave ample evidence of mature instinct.　Without that, the spiritual discoveries in "Bound East for Cardiff," in "The Straw" and many other plays would never have been made.　But the purely emotional attitude was distinctly that of a child, angry at being thwarted, violently self-assertive, supremely self-centered, imperious and impish at the same time, plunging easily from premature exaltation to despair, almost utterly lacking in compassion, and seldom attaining a mood of serenity.

In the plays that follow "All God's Chillun," the same emotional characteristics persist, but on a different plane, more terrifying at times because of their greater intensity, but richer in content.　The writing of "All God's Chillun" was, in effect, an act of humility which created a new perspective for the next stage in the poet's long journey. It was perhaps an act of exaggerated humility in overcompensation for the demonic pride of "Welded," and therefore less valuable as a means to inner harmony than a more quiet and reasoned self-appraisal would have been. But it was sufficient to mark the end of one series of troubled dreams and of the days of poetic youth. The future was to hold problems of more heroic proportions and of deeper tragedy illuminated, from time to time, by a correspondingly clearer spiritual insight.

PART TWO — *REGRESSION*

XV

"DESIRE UNDER THE ELMS"

Dragons of Youth

IN much of Greek tragedy, as well as in northern mythology, such as the Niebelungen cycle, the theme of incest is predominant. In its poetic expression, this theme quite evidently has implications far broader than its literal meaning. In spite of such tawdry phrases as "Œdipus complex," drawn from a nebulous jargon of certain early schools of psychiatry, and implying an acutely personal problem of neurotic individuals, the incest problem as we find it in the great tragedies and the enduring myths seems to symbolize very clearly a critical stage in the break between childhood and manhood. It is a moment of fateful hesitancy just beyond adolescence when the soft irresponsibility of childhood and its egotistical little empire become an enthralling dream from which it is exceedingly hard to awake to harsh realities.

In this larger sense, the apparently innocuous legend of

Peter Pan, the boy who did not want to grow up, takes its place among the legends of fateful regression. If, instead of desiring passionately to remain a child, Peter had been hounded by an inner will to grow up, we might have had a very different kind of story—a story of struggle against "monsters" that seemed to block his advance at every turn, against the temptation to return to the softly protecting mother principle that had previously stood between him and the clash of the outside world. In short, we should have had an "incest" story in its true psychological and poetic sense as distinct from its distorted personal sense. In mythology, the incest theme is generally used as the prelude to the development of a "hero," that is, of a man who has at last become strong enough to stand on his own feet and fight the obstacles of a real world. Later on, Christianity was to find in sacrifice and suffering and self-discipline the true prelude to the rebirth of the soul, free from the comtamination of the incest symbol. The Christian saints were to find in the Cross and in the idea of death to the old self the all-sufficient road to a spiritual resurrection, and the Christian poets, for the most part, were to use the same high symbols of purgation. But Greek tragedy was for centuries, and still is to a large extent, the model for the "hero" theme in the theatre, and this fact is of the utmost importance if we are to appraise correctly several of Eugene O'Neill's most important plays in that second period following the writing of "All God's Chillun."

We must remember that in "All God's Chillun," the poet accepted himself at last as intellectually a man, but still enslaved to the emotional and creative instincts of a child. Clearly, then, the next great struggle of the soul — unlike the sentimental contentment in childhood of Peter Pan — would be to seek maturity and reality, and to battle it out with all the inner obstacles seeking to prolong the alluring state of childhood. In spite of Jim Harris' brave words, "I'll play right up to the gates of Heaven with you," the stern fact remained that the soul could not find its heaven, its true inner harmony, in "play." More was needed. The emotions as well as the intellect and the understanding must throw off completely the desire to turn back to protecting motherly arms and a world of make-believe. O'Neill chose to express the idea of this struggle in the terms and symbols of Greek incest tragedy, and the first play of this new struggle was called "Desire Under the Elms."

Nothing could explain more clearly the exact implications of this play than O'Neill's description of the elm trees brooding over the Cabot farmhouse in New England in which the entire action takes place. These two enormous elms "bend their trailing branches down over the roof. They appear to protect and at the same time subdue. There is a sinister maternity in their aspect, a crushing jealous absorption. They have developed from their intimate contact with the life of man in the house an appalling humanness. They brood oppressively over

the house.   They are like exhausted women resting their
sagging breasts and hands and hair on its roof, and when
it rains their tears trickle down monotonously and rot on
the shingles."

If O'Neill had intended to write a sordid story of crime
on an isolated New England farm, such a description as
the above would have been totally unnecessary and irrele-
vant.   But he was not writing an ordinary story of sordid
crime.   He was writing a play of extraordinary emotional
intensity in which, consciously or unconsciously, he was
using the incest formula of Greek tragedy to express that
first terrific battle of the soul to escape from its own chains
to childhood.   In such a mood, every symbol associated
with childhood becomes "sinister" — much as the encompassing sea appeared sinister to old Chris.   For the time
being, there is no distinction between tender and strength-
giving motherhood, on the one hand, and on the other
the "sinister maternity" from which the soul seeks escape.
The very fact of the desire to escape completely distorts
the perspective.   The loving arms of a moment ago become in an instant the crushing absorbing arms of something sinister and appalling.   The real change is entirely
within the soul of the poet — a new attitude which becomes all the more intense because the desire to escape
is thwarted by an almost equally intense desire to remain.
The core of the tragedy in this first play of the second
stage lies in this — that the desire of the soul to remain
in its prison conquers, for the moment, the desire to escape.

Unless the play is understood in this perspective, and in this profound relationship to the pagan symbols of similar soul struggles, it loses all meaning in the scheme of the poet's quest.

The main characters of "Desire Under the Elms" are old Ephraim Cabot, hard fisted and stony hearted owner of the old farm, who frequently confuses himself with an "old testament" God, Whom he believes to be both hard and lonesome; Simeon and Peter Cabot, Ephraim's sons by a first wife; Eben Cabot, his son by a second wife, now dead, from whom he inherited the farm; and Abbie Putnam, a proud and possessive younger woman whom Ephraim brings back to the farm as his third wife, to the consternation of his sons, who see their inheritance threatened. Although old Ephraim Cabot dominates the entire play, and is felt when not seen, it is Eben who is the dramatic hero, who becomes the symbol of youth seeking escape, only to find itself hopelessly entangled in old yearnings. The very first description of him gives the key to his character. "His face is well formed, good-looking, but its expression is resentful and defensive. His defiant, dark eyes remind one of a wild animal's in captivity. Each day is a cage in which he finds himself trapped but inwardly unsubdued. There is a fierce repressed vitality about him." In other words, he is O'Neill's equivalent of the young Siegfried in the dwarf's cave — or of Orestes driven on by the furies.

But O'Neill's equivalent of these mythological heroes is

of a very different texture from the originals, wholly without the benefit of mythological proportions. Eben Cabot is the personification of youthful lust driven on by devotion to his dead mother's image and the suppressed rage he feels at her early death, which he believes was brought on by his father's cruelty. He believes the farm to be rightly his, because it was his mother's before him ; his father, in his eyes, is an interloper and a robber, fit only to be hated and cheated at every turn. When Eben goes brutally to a notorious woman in the village, it is revenge as well as lust that drives him, because he has heard that his father once knew this woman too. He boasts of it to his brothers : "She may've been his'n — and your'n, too — but she's mine now ! . . . The p'int is she was his'n — and now she b'longs t' me !" So deeply has Eben identified himself with his mother's wrongs that his every act is motivated in large part by the desire for revenge on his father. The older brothers resent old Ephraim, too, but for a simpler reason. He has driven them like slaves, made them hedge their lives around with the stone fences lifted from the rebellious soil, and given them nothing in exchange. In sudden rebellion, when they hear their father has married again, thus destroying their last chance of inheriting the farm, they leave for the California gold hills, making over their worthless shares in the farm to Eben in exchange for Ephraim's hidden hoard of gold which Eben discloses to them. In Eben's mind, the gold was the result of his mother's slavery and death — it belongs to his mother and to him !

With this setting of suppressed desires and distorted passions we are fully prepared for the consequences of Ephraim's third marriage to a young wife. At first, Eben resents her furiously as an intruder in his mother's place. Then he succumbs to his attraction toward her youth and coarse beauty and to the same frantic feeling he held toward the woman in the village — to make his own everything that his father has possessed. The play becomes a three-cornered battle, for imperious domination by the father, for the destruction of the father by the son, and for the possession of the farm and all else by Abbie. Abbie is described as "thirty-five, buxom, full of vitality. Her round face is pretty but marred by its rather gross sensuality. There is strength and obstinacy in her jaw, a hard determination in her eyes, and about her whole personality the same unsettled, untamed, desperate quality which is so apparent in Eben." Ephraim Cabot, in contrast, is described as "seventy-five, tall and gaunt, with great, wiry, concentrated power, but stoop-shouldered from toil. His face is as hard as if it were hewn out of a boulder, yet there is a weakness in it, a petty pride in his own narrow strength. His eyes are small, close together, and extremely near-sighted, blinking continually in the effort to focus on objects, their stare having a straining, ingrowing quality."

It is well worth noting at this point a strong character-istic of O'Neill's method, particularly evident in his later plays, of dealing with evil.   He does not romanticize it. He is blunt to the point of brutality in describing evil pas-sions, whether those of lust or pride or possessiveness. But even though the motivations he gives his characters may explain their evil actions, they are not motivations that seek to excuse, palliate or romanticize the evil they bring.   Abbie's face is "marred" by her gross sen-suality.   The criticism is always valid that the grosser forms of evil need not be depicted on the stage — that drama, after the Greek fashion, can deal with the conse-quences of evil rather than with the description of evil itself.   But once an author makes the decision to depict evil at all in the body of his play, the whole question of the integrity of his work from that point on depends on a complete discarding of that oily, narcotic deception of pretending that good and evil are one and the same, to be distinguished only by custom or convention.   With such a premise, the whole core of serious drama vanishes, and with it all sense of the spiritual integrity which is the hall mark of the true poet.

From her first appearance on the farm, Abbie takes deep and full possession of everything, including Eben, who becomes at once, in her eyes, a means to an end — further undisputed possession of all that Eben holds dear.   To this end she tries to gain his sympathy by telling him of her own hard life, and to gain his affection by pointed ref-

erence to the youth they share. At first, Eben tries furiously to resist his growing feeling for her. "I'm fightin'
him — I'm fightin' yew," he tells her defiantly, "fightin'
fur Maw's rights t' her hum! An' I'm onto ye. Ye
hain't foolin' me a mite. Ye're aimin' t' swaller up everythin' an' make it your'n. Waal, you'll find I'm a heap
sight bigger hunk nor yew kin chew!"

In the meantime, old Ephraim begins to develop a curious tolerance of the "softness" he sees in Eben, and Abbie
begins to be frightened. What if Ephraim, who feels
he is getting old and "ripe on the bow," should decide to
leave the farm to Eben instead of to her? But when she
taunts him with the idea, Ephraim's own petty pride rises
up. "If I could, in my dyin' hour," he says, "I'd set it
afire an' watch it burn — this house an' every ear o' corn
an' every tree down to the last blade o' hay! I'd sit an'
know it was all a-dying with me an' no one else'd ever own
what was mine, what I'd made out o' nothin' with my own
sweat 'n' blood!" Then he adds: "'Ceptin' the cows.
Them I'd turn free." And when Abbie asks harshly
what he would do with her, he replies, none too reassur-
ingly, "Ye'd be turned free, too." This scene leads to her
discovery that what Ephraim most desires in the world is
another son, that if Abbie can bring him this last blessing on
his old age, he will give her anything she asks, even the
farm.

This discovery only strengthens Abbie's determination
to make Eben love her — to be more than ever the means

to her great possessive end. She plays upon his love for
his mother, covers her evil desires with a veneer of
mother love, and finally, in the parlor of the house, the
room in which Eben's mother was laid out before burial,
she persuades him that in loving her he is only revenging
his mother's death. Thus Eben, by the false road of an
incestuous love, thinks he has discovered freedom from
the softness and humiliation of his youthful resentment.

But Eben's false sense of freedom is short lived.
Within a year, Abbie has a son by Eben — but Eben finds
once more that his father stands above him. "I don't like
this," he exclaims. "I don't like lettin' on what's mine is
his'n. I been doin' that all my life. I'm gettin' t' the
end of b'arin' it!" Abbie's efforts to comfort him, her
assurances that "somethin's bound t' happen" are of no
avail. The seed of dark evil has been sown, and Eben is
beginning to watch the strange plant grow.

It is old Ephraim, boastful and derisive in what he
believes to be his new fatherhood, who strikes the second
blow at Eben. He gloats over the boy, and then tells
him that Abbie always despised him, and wanted to have
a son only to make sure that she and not Eben would have
the farm. In a rage, Eben attacks his father and the two
men struggle until Abbie rushes out to separate them.
Then, when his father has gone, Eben vents his rage on
Abbie — tells her what he has heard, and refuses to believe her wild protests that she really loves him now,
and that all she once said was simply in resentment when

he hated and ignored her. As for his son, "I wish he
never was born!" cries Eben. "I wish he'd die this minit!
I wish I'd never sot eyes on him! It's him — yew havin'
him — a-purpose t' steal — that's changed everythin'!"
When Abbie pleads that she might make it "'s if he'd
never come up between us," Eben answers bitterly, "But
ye hain't God, be ye?" As he leaves her, threatening
never to see her again, Abbie, who does love Eben now
with a tortured intensity, says strangely, "Mebbe I kin
take back one thin' God does!" The tragedy sweeps on.
To prove her love for Eben, Abbie kills her new-born son!

She comes to Eben to tell him what she has done. At
first he thinks she has killed his father, and takes a sort of
grim delight in the idea, but when he at last understands that it is his son who has been killed — the one
thing really his in the world — a new rage sweeps over
him. "I kin see why ye done it!" he yells, "'cause ye
wanted t' steal agen — steal the last thin' ye'd left me —
my part o' him — no, the hull o' him — ye saw he looked
like me — ye knowed he was all mine — an' ye couldn't
bar it — I know ye! Ye killed him fur bein' mine!"
He rushes off to get the Sheriff.

Then comes Abbie's complete confession to old Ephraim
— Eben's frantic return to Abbie, whom he still loves in
spite of himself — his plea that they run away together
before the Sheriff comes, and Abbie's calm statement:
"I got t' take my punishment — t' pay fur my sin." But
it is the sin of murder, and not her love for Eben that

she means. "I don't repent that sin!" she says proudly,
"as if defying God." When the sheriff comes, Eben
gives himself up as a partner in the crime— his one and
only act of true manliness. Even old Ephraim gives him
one look of grudging admiration. "Purty good—fur
yew!" he exclaims—and then goes off to follow the pre-
cepts of his peculiar god—"God's lonesome, hain't He?
God's hard an' lonesome!"

In many respects, "Desire Under the Elms" is unlike
all O'Neill's other plays in its complete absorption in the
sins of lust, and in its description of those sins—proudly
unrepented to the end. In this lies its sense of almost
overwhelming defeat. Using the incest symbol of old
mythology and tragedy to describe the first battle of youth
against the ties of childhood, it describes a battle without
an outcome. Eben is victorious in only one thing—a
final acceptance of one responsibility of manhood. But
he goes off to prison with Abbie, still loving her—the
person who has symbolized his mother in his antagonism
to his father. The feminine tie to childhood is still as
much a part of the poet's struggle as in the closing scenes
of "All God's Chillun." Only the masculine side begins
to break free, no longer with the idea of "playing right
up to the gates of Heaven," but with the serious purpose
of accepting full responsibility for the realities of life
and the consequences of evil deed. Eben, at the close
of the play, is no longer living in a world of make-believe.

But the feminine side of the poet's soul is still mightily

in possession — and again, the child born of that longing
for the childish past cannot live.   It is killed — by the
woman, the symbol of the sheltering maternity, now
turned "sinister," to which the child can never return if
he wishes to become wholly a man.   The brooding elms
retain their appalling quality.   The desire bred under
them is an unholy desire, from which Eben is not yet
free.   It is not difficult to know that the Ebens of future
plays will be driven by the fates and furies within their
souls, demanding the price of redemption.

But, of course, as we know, every character in such a
play represents a part of the poet's soul — one of those
countless voices of tumult which must some day be resolved into a harmony.   Ephraim Cabot is also part of the
complex struggle — the near-sighted one, of narrow vision
and narrow pride, imperious, yet in many ways completely
a man, identifying himself with a lonesome and hard God.
We must reckon with that quality, too, in the poet's soul
— the overharsh and unforgiving judge of his own weaknesses, all too likely to drive him from one compensating
extreme to another, unless a true woman, like Maria de
Cordova, in "The Fountain," can bring him "tenderness."
Of the "dreamer," we would expect to hear less and less
— for the manhood in Eben has grown up.   But of the
proud, imperious thinker, there is too much left.   Then,
too, there are the brothers to be heard from — the
brothers who, like Andrew in "Beyond the Horizon," were
able to break away in a search for wealth.   The strange

persistency of all of these qualities of soul is not the least amazing quality in a play so utterly different from all earlier plays in texture and treatment and immediate theme as "Desire Under the Elms."

This play will always be subject to the criticism of being too brutal and realistic a treatment of a universal theme which the classic dramatists have always approached with a grandiose and coldly symbolic attitude. It is a torrential outpouring of crude feeling, almost terrifying in its raw projection upon a realistic stage. But aside from this aspect—admittedly a very important one in a purely dramatic discussion of O'Neill's work—the meaning of the play as an integral part of the long struggle of a poet's soul toward inner harmony should be accepted at its own worth. It is the first great struggle to emerge into maturity. The significance of its failure can only be measured in the light of renewed conflicts to come and of their greater measure of achievement.

XVI

"MARCO MILLIONS"

The Missing Soul

In the closing scenes of "Marco Millions," some of the characters wear masks. In his next play, "The Great God Brown," O'Neill uses for the first time the complete technique of the mask. There is more than casual and accidental importance to this growing desire for the use of masks. It is an integral part of the struggle which followed the naked revelations of the first fight for maturity in "Desire Under the Elms." The spirit of "Marco Millions" throughout is that of a spiritual mask— a covering up of the teeming and terrifying emotions revealed in "Desire Under the Elms" by a spirit of mockery and derision, through which there break only in rare and beautiful moments the tenderness and compassion faintly foreshadowed in "The Fountain."

"Marco Millions" has been called a comedy and a satire. This is true—in part. But beneath its irony and its mockery, the very sad eyes of the poet's soul peer forth. It is a play of deep and insatiable hunger, of dark questioning and of ineffable tenderness. The pos-

sessed soul of Eben Cabot, as it were, turns to the East —
that ever-brooding symbol of spiritual maternity — as if,
wearied after the first raw outburst of passions under the
sinister elms, he might hope to find in spiritual and philosophical regression the answer that brings peace and freedom from all further conflict with reality. But he finds
there once more the lonely spirit of Ephraim Cabot, now
softened and humbled into the dignified person of Kublai
Kaan ; he finds also his greedy brothers, not as California
gold hunters, but as the brothers of Polo and the fusion
of their natures in the self-sufficient son and nephew,
Marco Polo ; he finds, too, that feminine soul of a child,
lost since the writing of "All God's Chillun," which must
always be with him until it grows in beauty and strength
and can become, in a sense, his own soul's beauty and
tender strength. The Princess Kukachin, the "little
flower" of the great Kaan, is this tender soul, over whose
body, in death, the Kaan can weep and say, "I think you
are hiding your eyes, Kukachin. You are a little girl
again. You are playing hide and seek. You are pretending. Did we not once play such games together, you
and I ? You have made your face still, you have made
your face cold, you have set your lips in a smile so remote
— you are pretending even that you are dead !" Yes —
"playing right up to the gates of Heaven," even in death.
This might have been a cry from the tortured spirit of Jim
Harris, as it is certainly a cry from the poet, yearning for
the soul he must have before he can discover peace.

There is no "Eben" in "Marco Millions." There is no need of one. It is a play in which the poet himself steps out as commentator, before the stage, on the other parts of himself in masked and unhappy or uncouth parade. Some plays are like that. In their whole structure and method, they are author's comments. The hero is the singer of the song, and the play is only his mask and his concealment. "Marco Millions" is, in this sense, the most completely masked play O'Neill has ever written — just as "Desire Under the Elms" is, up to this point, at least, the most completely unmasked play. It is almost inevitable that one should have followed the other, as great rage is followed by exceedingly great reserve.

Yet "Marco Millions," by the very fact of its masked expression, is thoroughly revealing of the second stage of spiritual conflict through which the poet must have been passing at this time. The figure of Marco, seen at first writing immature poetry to Donata, a Venetian girl of twelve, and then carried through all the fantastic stages of extraverted action and bawdy greed, is no more than a summation of that familiar part of himself seen in so many of the poet's earlier plays. Marco, in short, is one of those "brothers" whose conflicting natures emerged in the very first full length play — and continue, as a recurring theme, long after they have apparently been forgotten in other and greater turmoils. Once more, it is no casual accident that this reappearance of the Andrew Mayo personality should appear faintly, at first, in "De-

sire Under the Elms" — as old themes recur faintly in a
new movement of one symphony — to be followed by
more insistent repetition in "Marco Millions," and then,
in the very next play, "The Great God Brown," as the
completely dominant theme, with masks, and with an ultimate fusion of the two personalities of Bill Brown and
Dion Anthony in one person.

It is a more mature Robert Mayo, however — just as
it is a more mature Eben Cabot — who, in the words and
emphasis of the playwright throws bitter scorn on the
Marco-Andrew in "Marco Millions." The playwright
has become, through suffering, a Robert who can be
amused as well as disgusted by the antics of his greedy
and active "brother." Marco Polo is a partly likable
scoundrel, the natural product of his practical, mercantile and acquisitive forbears. His father and uncle take
him on a long voyage to the East. Before going, he
promises to be forever faithful to the little Donata, and,
in a manner of speaking he keeps his promise — returning
after twenty years to marry a fat and bovine Donata, and
to shower vast wealth, the symbol of his very modern
mercantile success, before the eyes of his fellow Venetians.
His infidelities with the ladies of the East have been, so
he feels, of a very obvious nature, and have not in the
least involved his affections. Since his conscience is a
highly obtuse affair, if it exists at all, he feels quite satisfied with himself as a keeper of promises over the years!

But what of the Princess Kukachin? Her grand-

father, Kublai Kaan, had requested the brothers Polo to
bring back with them one hundred wise men from the
West, selected by the Pope, to debate with his own wise
men of the East. But the Pope, with a not-unconscious
irony, has preferred to let the brothers Polo take their
bumptious nephew back to the court of the Kaan, rather
than the wise men, and with these cryptic instructions
(having seen Marco in the flesh): "Let him set an example of virtuous Western manhood, amid all the levities
of paganism, shun the frailty of poetry, have a million to
his credit, as he so beautifully phrased it, and I will
wager a million of something or other myself that the
Kaan will soon be driven to seek spiritual salvation somewhere! Mark my words, Marco will be worth a million
wise men—in the cause of wisdom!" But the exquisite
irony of the Pope's instructions is, of course, utterly lost
on the brothers Polo and on Marco. The brothers can
only gurgle: "Mark is making a good impression already!" and "Well, he's got a head on him!", and Marco
can only "begin to swell out a bit matter-of-factly" and
say, "Never mind about me. When do we start?" He
cannot yet, however, leave behind him the curious poem
which began so well and ended in the "million to his
credit" which had so highly amused the wise Pope. He
tries to throw it away, calling himself "a damn fool," but
picks it up again as he rushes forth to join his respectable
uncles. It is almost the last time that he exhibits the
faintest trace of having a "soul"—yet it is in a passionate

search for that lost trace of his soul that the little Princess Kukachin at last dies of a broken heart !

O'Neill introduces many minor themes into the story of Marco Polo's voyage to the Far East, most of them having to do with his personal ideas of comparative religions and comparative civilizations, which touch only vaguely on the main theme of Marco's lost soul. At such moments, when the "ambitious thinker" is uppermost in the poet's consciousness, the true poetic sweep, gathering its force from intuition and feeling, disappears into an almost pedantic comment, based on ideas which the thinker happens to hold at the moment. The prostitute, for example, appears in one civilization after another, but always as the same person, and as a dual symbol of man's earthly desires and of the strange motherhood he is seeking in all nature. There is nothing new in the use of this dual symbol, and certain modern psychologists have taken it up avidly, yet it seems to be in origin largely a concept of the introverted East and to have about it that strange duplicity by which men seek to exonerate themselves through a pleasant fiction. Each successive civilization is also presented in identical symbols, with the ruler flanked on one side by the military and on the other by the religious sign of authority, and by all ages of men. In all of this, however, the three Polos see only trade and profits. As western "Christians" they have utterly lost contact with the oriental springs of their own religion.

They are Christian in name but children of materialistic greed in heart and mind.

The Polos remain many long years at the court of the Great Kaan, Marco achieving many modern wonders of extraverted energy and accomplishment, including the introduction of paper money and the use of gunpowder for cannon, as well as onerous and productive measures of taxation on the necessities rather than the luxuries of life. In an easy, off-hand way, he is kind to the little Princess Kukachin, who, to the utter dismay of Kublai Kaan, falls in love with him. When the Kaan insists on asking Marco, from year to year, about the condition of his immortal soul, and receives consistently less and less evidence of its effective existence, it is Kukachin alone who retains a belief that it is still there. She has little enough to go on, but she bears this much witness to its existence : "I have seen it — once," she says proudly, "when he bound up my dog's leg, once when he played with a slave's baby, once when he listened to music over water and I heard him sigh, once when he looked at sunrise, another time at sunset, another at the stars, another at the moon, and each time he said that Nature was wonderful. And all the while, whenever he has been near me I have always felt — something strange and different — and that something must be His Honor's soul, must it not ?"

When the unhappy Kukachin finds that she is destined to be married to a Persian Prince, she asks that the Polos, being masters of navigation, may conduct her to her fateful destination. The Kaan grudgingly grants her request, having a premonition of her tragedy. His parting with her is a deep sorrow, filled with compassion. "We have said all we can say. Little Daughter, all rare things are secrets which cannot be revealed to anyone. That is why life must be so lonely. But I love you more dearly than anything on earth. And I know you love me. So perhaps we do not need to understand." He leaves her before Marco appears in the full glory of a new admiral's uniform. "I must fly in retreat," he says, "from what I can neither laugh away nor kill. Write when you reach Persia. Tell me—all you can tell—particularly what his immortal soul is like!" But the Kaan's ancient spiritual advisor, Chu-Yin, takes it upon himself to give a final admonition to Marco in the Kaan's name. "You are, at some time every day of the voyage," he tells the bumptious admiral, "to look carefully and deeply into the Princess's eyes and note what you see there." Will Marco perhaps see in her love for him the soul he needs for his salvation? His reply to Chu-Yin is not encouraging. "What for?" he asks, and then, brightly, "Oh, he's afraid she'll get fever in the tropics. Well, you tell him I'll see to it she keeps in good condition. I'll do what's right by her without considering fear or favor. Then, of course, if her husband thinks at the end of the voyage that my work deserves a bonus—why, that's up to him." Poor little Kukachin!

The voyage to Persia lasts nearly two years, during which Marco saves Kukachin from drowning, defends her against pirates and nurses her through a long fever. But he never discovers the secret in her eyes. At last, in the Persian harbor of Hormuz, she almost brings him to see her as a woman and to know her love — but he tells her that it is Donata he has seen in her eyes. "Yes. Here she is!" he exclaims enthusiastically, drawing a miniature of Donata from his breast pocket, "The future Mrs. Marco Polo! You may believe it or not but like a flash she was standing there in your place and I was talking to her, not you at all!" Poor little Kukachin! Poor immortal soul of Marco Polo!

Kukachin dies in her lonely exile. The aged Kaan sees in a crystal the portent of her death — and then summons up the vision of Marco's return to Venice — the welcome, the feast, the blaze of riches, the betrothal to the fat and middle-aged Donata, and Marco's speech to the busily eating Venetians upon the millions upon millions of capital invested in the silk business of the East in which "there are constantly employed millions upon millions upon millions of millions of worms!" Then, in the ensuing darkness, comes the voice of the Great Kaan in pitying scorn of the Venetians' parody on Christianity. "The Word became their flesh, they say. Now all is flesh! And can their flesh become the Word again?"

The play closes with the bringing home of Kukachin. Over her, the Great Kaan utters a prayer — but Chu-Yin tells him it was the prayer of his pride and his power, the prayer of the imperious one. "Weep, old man," Chu-Yin tells him compassionately, "Be humble and weep for your child. The old should cherish sorrow." And then the old man, humble at last in his grief, bends over Kukachin's body, summoning her to awake. "Take the blindfold from my dim eyes," he beseeches her. "Whisper your secret in my ear. I—I am dead and you are living! Weep for me, Kukachin! Weep for the dead!" His tears come. "I bid you welcome home, Little Flower! I bid you welcome home!"

Thus the gift of tenderness, sent by the dying prayer of Maria de Cordova to Ponce de Leon, reaches the poet's soul at last, and with it compassion. The child, Kukachin, is no more, but her spirit can now be reborn, to live again in strength and the beauty of creation.

But the spirit of Marco Polo is still among the millions upon millions of worms, eating out the heart of western civilization, battening on greed, hard, defiant, crafty, a mask of the outer man. In his next play, "The Great God Brown," the poet was to reveal the secret of masks— protective faces against reality—a last defense of youth against maturity and wisdom.

XVII

"THE GREAT GOD BROWN"

Divine Laughter

IN "The Great God Brown," two major themes of the
search for inner harmony unite — the conflict of the
brothers, begun in "Beyond the Horizon," and the yearning for maternal protection against the real world.
Although Dion Anthony and William Brown are not
brothers in the flesh, they represent the same opposing
principles as Robert and Andrew Mayo — subjective instability against objective downrightness. They are the
sons of two partners in a contracting and building firm.
They and all of the characters of the play wear masks,
representing their life attitudes as contrasted with their
real inner feelings. Dion wears the mask of Pan as a
protection against the world, but has the soul of an ascetic
— Dionysius and Saint Anthony, as it were. Brown wears
no mask at first, when he is still at ease with realities.
But later, like a new Marco Polo who realizes that he has
lost his soul, he seeks the missing part of his life by ap-
propriating Dion's mask of Pan after Dion has died.
After this, Brown lives two lives, his own and that of

Dion, and no one else, not even Dion's wife, realizes that Dion is actually dead.   In this way, O'Neill indicates that the two men are really one person.   In the end, the new Brown-Anthony seeks protection from the harshness of life in the arms of a symbolic maternity, only to discover at last a greater reality in God.

"The Great God Brown" is perhaps a better reading than acting play.   In the theatrical sense, O'Neill was embarking upon a new and dangerous experiment in deciding to use masks which his characters could put on or remove as the emotions of the particular scene demanded. It was a different technique even from that of the old Greek theatre, and destined to cause confusion in the mind of audiences rather than to clarify the many complex situations.   The idea was more ingenious than its execution.   In reading the play, however, if one is willing to consider the two men as two sides of one person, rather than as separate individuals, the dramatic meaning becomes clearer.

In the prologue, we are re-introduced at once to the Polo family.   Billy Brown's father "is fifty or more, the type of bustling, genial, successful, provincial business man, stout and hearty," — Marco Polo, perhaps, a couple of decades after his return to Venice.   Brown's mother "is a dumpy woman of forty-five, overdressed in black lace and spangles" — Donata.   Billy Brown himself "is a handsome, tall and athletic boy of nearly eighteen. He is blond and blue-eyed, with a likeable smile and a frank

good-humored face, its expression already indicating a
disciplined restraint.   His manner has the easy self-assur-
ance of a normal intelligence," — let us say, Marco Polo
Junior.   The mother is defiant and possessive, holding
both husband and son firmly to her ambitious will.   Billy
must become an architect and expand the scope of the firm
of Anthony and Brown.   But she does find the June
nights and the moonlight colder than they used to be —
the moonlight, she remembers, was warm and beautiful
in her youth.

The prologue also introduces us to the Anthonys.   The
father, a relic of Ephraim Cabot, "is a tall lean man of
fifty-five or sixty with a grim, defensive face, obstinate to
the point of stupid weakness."   The mother, who might
well have been Eben Cabot's mother, "is a thin, frail, faded
woman, her manner perpetually nervous and distraught,
but with a sweet and gentle face that had once been beautiful."   Following them along the embankment of the
lake, "as if he were a stranger, walking alone, is their son,
Dion.   He is about the same height as young Brown but
lean and wiry, without repose, continually in restless nervous movement.   His face is masked.   The mask is a
fixed forcing of his own face — dark, spiritual, poetic,
passionately super-sensitive, helplessly unprotected in its
childlike, religious faith in life — into the expression of a
mocking, reckless, defiant, gayly scoffing and sensual young
Pan."

The father and mother have heard that Bill Brown is to

be an architect. Their own ambition must be satisfied by
having Dion, too, become an architect and "a better architect than Brown's boy or I'll turn you out in the gutter
without a penny!" storms the father. The mother keeps
harping back to the fact that Dion "always painted pictures
so well." Dion, wearing his mask, is scornful and mocking. "I thank Mr. Anthony," he says, "for this splendid
opportunity to create myself — in my mother's image, so
she may feel her life comfortably concluded." The elder
Anthonys, like the Browns, also find the June nights
colder than they used to be, and go indoors.

Then we are introduced to Margaret — who loves Dion
as she sees him with his mask of Pan. Bill Brown tries
to propose to her, but her mind is wholly given up to her
image of Dion. "Dion is the moon and I'm the sea. I
want to feel the moon kissing the sea. I want Dion to
leave the sky to me . . . Dion! Margaret! Peggy!
Peggy is Dion's girl — Peggy is Dion's little girl" — once
more this theme from "All God's Chillun" — and then,
"Dion is my Daddy-O!", followed by a growingly maternal and possessive note, "And I'll be Mrs. Dion —
Dion's wife — and he'll be my Dion — my own Dion —
my baby! The moon is drowned in the tides of my
heart, and peace sinks deep through the sea!"

The real Dion Anthony can never appear unmasked
before this possessive, maternal Margaret — for it is that
very maternity, sinister like the elms, which he is fighting
to escape. "Why was I born without a skin, O God," he

cries out when alone and unmasked, "that I must wear
armor in order to touch or to be touched ?"   When Billy
Brown tells Dion that Margaret loves him, Dion, once
more left alone, cries exultantly, "She protects me !   Her
arms are softly around me !   She is warmly around me !
She is my skin !   She is my armor !   Now I am born —
I — the I ! — one and indivisible — I who love Margaret !" and looking triumphantly at his mask, "You are
outgrown !   I am beyond you !   O God, now I believe !"
But when Margaret comes upon him thus, without his
mask, she does not know him.   She thinks he is a stranger.
He has to clap on his mask of Pan again before she can
know and love him.

The details of the play are of less interest than the
growth of the masks and their effect upon the individuals.
Dion and Margaret are destined never to know each other.
It is only the Pan mask which she loves — a mask which
becomes more and more Mephistophelian as the play
progresses, while the real Anthony underneath the mask
becomes more and more of an ascetic, desperately searching for God.   But what are the reasons for Anthony's
mask of Dion ?   What is there in common between the
naked and unmasked Eben of "Desire Under the Elms,"
and the Anthony, still seeking escape, but accepting a false
love under a mask ?   Twice — and both times to Brown
— Anthony explains, and in those explanations we can
find the whole of the poet's inner conflict.

"One day when I was four years old," Dion tells

Brown, "a boy sneaked up behind when I was drawing a
picture in the sand he couldn't draw and hit me on the
head with a stick and kicked out my picture and laughed
when I cried.   It wasn't what he'd done that made me
cry, but him !   I had loved and trusted him and suddenly
the good God was disproved in his person and the evil and
injustice of Man was born !   Everyone called me cry-
baby, so I became silent for life and designed a mask of
the Bad Boy Pan in which to live and rebel against that
other boy's God and protect myself from His cruelty.
And that other boy, secretly he felt ashamed but he
couldn't acknowledge it ; so from that day he instinctively
developed into the good boy, the good friend, the good
man, William Brown !"   This Dion says with his mask
on.

In contrast, he has this to say to Brown with his mask
off : "What aliens we were to each other !" (He is speaking now of his father.)   "When he lay dead, his face
looked so familiar that I wondered where I had met that
man before.   Only at the second of my conception.   After
that, we grew hostile with concealed shame.   And my
mother ?   I remember a sweet, strange girl, with affec-
tionate, bewildered eyes as if God had locked her in a
dark closet without any explanation.   I was the sole doll
our ogre, her husband, allowed her and she played mother
and child with me for many years in that house until at
last through two years I watched her die with the shy

pride of one who has lengthened her dress and put up her
hair.   And I felt like a forsaken toy and cried to be
buried with her, because her hands alone had caressed
without clawing.   She lived long and aged greatly in
the two days before they closed her coffin.   The last time
I looked, her purity had forgotten me, she was stainless
and imperishable, and I knew my sobs were ugly and
meaningless to her virginity ; so I shrank away, back into
life, with naked nerves jumping like fleas, and in due
course of nature another girl called me her boy in the
moon and married me and became three mothers in one
person, while I got paint on my paws in an endeavor to
see God ! "

Two things, then, determined the character of the mask
—the desire to escape the buffets of the real world, its
meannesses and its jealousies, as summed up in Bill
Brown's blow at the age of four, and the desire, against
his own better nature and his quest of maturity, to become
the Bad Boy Pan, who could play the child and be loved
by the possessive, maternal feminine that would, if it
could, be the mother of all living, of Pan himself, the sea
swallowing up the moon in its tides.   At last we find the
union in the poet's soul of all the fears of earlier stages.
We find the enthralling maternal sea, the brutality of the
forecastle, possessiveness and envy, and the stubbornly
weak pride of the Old Testament father principle.   We
also find the explanation of all the defenses set up against

the fears, the unbridled Pan-like sensuality of Eben, accepting the child's position in love, the arrogance of Brutus Jones, the quivering shame and inferiority of Jim Harris, the frantic regression to the primitive in "The First Man" and "The Hairy Ape." We find the search for narcotic peace in the deep introversion of Kublai Kaan's Far East or in the soothing pantheistic image of "The Fountain." It would all become a picture of hopeless decadence were it not for the titanic driving will of the poet's soul to become free. We must not forget the dawn above the fog in "Bound East for Cardiff," the spirit of sacrifice beyond Robert Mayo's horizon, the splendid affirmation of life in "The Straw," and the acceptance of creation in "The First Man."

Dion Anthony, exhausted by dissipation, at last finds himself dying in Bill Brown's rooms. The Margaret who loved only the Dion mask has crushed him completely. It is only with Cybel, who wears a prostitute's mask to the world, but becomes the quiet wisdom of maternal friendship when with Anthony, that Dion has been able to discard his mask. Their relationship has been pure, because unmasked. It is Cybel who knows the ascetic Anthony — the one who reads the Imitation of Christ, by à Kempis, as a prayer for deliverance. "Keep thyself as a pilgrim, and a stranger upon earth, to whom the affairs of this world do not—belong! Keep thy heart free and raised upward to God because thou hast not here a lasting abode." But Brown, envious as when a small boy, has even tried to rob Anthony of Cybel, who, to him, of course, remains masked as the prostitute. In dying, Anthony tells Brown the truth, speaking from his mask : "Brown will still need me — to reassure him he's alive ! I've loved, lusted, won and lost, sung and wept ! I've been life's lover ! I've fulfilled her will and if she's through with me now it's only because I was too weak to dominate her in turn. It isn't enough to be her creature, you've got to create her or she requests you to destroy herself."

Then he taunts Brown with being neither creature nor creator. Brown has stolen part of Anthony's creative life, using his talents without giving him credit. "I've been the brains ! I've been the design !" cries Dion, "But Mr. Brown, the Great Brown, has no faith ! He couldn't design a cathedral without it looking like the First Supernatural Bank ! . . . Why has he never been able to love — since my Margaret ? Why has he never married ? Why has he tried to steal Cybel, as he once tried to steal Margaret ? Isn't it out of revenge — and envy ?" Then Dion makes his mocking last will and testament. "I leave Dion Anthony to William Brown — for him to love and obey — for him to become me — then my Margaret will love me — my children will love me — Mr. and Mrs. Brown and sons, happily ever after !" But before he dies, Anthony's mask falls off, and it is the Anthony, not the Dion, who repeats in his dying breath, "Our father who art in Heaven," and who cries out "Forgive

me, Billy. Bury me, hide me, forget me for your own
happiness! May Margaret love you! May you design the Temple of Man's Soul! Blessed are the meek
and the poor in spirit!"

But from the moment of Dion Anthony's death, Bill
Brown is forced, as by an inner and compelling fate, to
wear Dion's mask, to take Dion's place with Margaret and
her children, to be Brown at his office, but Dion at home,
and to lead the lives of both men fused into one. Margaret never knows that Anthony has died, and loves
Brown, now wearing the mask of Dion, more than she
ever loved Dion himself. But the wearing of the Pan-
like mask of Dion slowly kills Brown as it did Anthony.
The weakened Brown must now wear a mask of his own at
his office, as well as that of Dion when at home. At last,
in mocking irony, masked as Dion, he tells Margaret and
some clients who have come to the office that Brown is
dead, and then runs away, leaving them to suspect that
"Dion" has killed Brown. Margaret and the clients rush
into the next room and find — only Brown's mask. But
they do not know the difference. To them, the mask is
the whole person. They carry it out solemnly as if they
were carrying a corpse.

The police hunt for "Dion" and shoot him — wounding,
of course, the real Brown, who still wears Dion's mask.
But Cybel comes to his side before his death — and takes
off her own mask before him for the first time, so that he
can see her as she is underneath, no longer the prostitute,

but rather as a symbol of protecting mother earth. The dying Brown, throwing away the Dion mask, clings to her. "The earth is warm," he murmurs. But Cybel only soothes him. "Go to sleep, Billy," she whispers. "Yes, Mother," he answers, and later, "I'm getting sleepy. What's the prayer you taught me — Our Father — ?"

Cybel guides his words: "Our Father Who Art!" and Brown repeats in ecstasy "Who art! Who art! I know! I have found Him! I hear Him speak! 'Blessed are they that weep, for they shall laugh!' Only he that has wept can laugh!" And then, in an outburst of illumination, such as the poet has never expressed before, one which carries his soul to a new realization of the meaning of suffering and creation, Brown cries out: "The laughter of Heaven sows earth with a rain of tears, and out of Earth's transfigured birth-pain the laughter of Man returns to bless and play again in innumerable dancing gales of flame upon the knees of God!" With these words, and freed at last from both his own mask and that of Dion, William Brown dies.

But Margaret, who comes in just as Brown dies, does not see him. She sees in the room only the discarded mask of her Dion — of her lover, her husband — her boy! She kisses him (the mask of Dion) good-by, but tells him that he will live forever. "You will sleep under my heart! I will feel you stirring in your sleep, forever under my heart!" Until the end, then, Margaret remains the symbol of possession — of the woman who

would be the mother of all living, of Pan. It is Brown
and Anthony, the conflicting male symbols, now joined in
death, as they were linked together in life, who have discovered the laughter of heaven, and God, through the
torture and sufferings underneath their masked existence.

There is still no promised end to the poet's inner conflict, even in the illumination of Brown's dying words,
for, although the Man may have died to his masks, the
Woman still cherishes the mask, and promises it life
forever, under her heart.   O'Neill's next play was to continue the conflict in these very terms. In "Lazarus
Laughed," it is Lazarus alone who does not wear a mask.
He alone, brought back from the dead, knows the laughter
of Heaven born of Man's pain. It is only that part of
the poet's soul which has won partial freedom. Tiberius
Caesar is masked, the imperious one, and so is Caligula,
the cruel one, and Miriam, the wife of Lazarus, who
grows old as he grows young. And the symbols of mankind of all ages and sexes are masked. For mankind has
as it were, carried off the mask of Bill Brown, thinking
it to be Brown himself, and Margaret has taken the mask
of Dion under her heart.

There is also the weakness of self-exoneration to be
purged from the poet's soul. The sufferings of Dion
Anthony have come from the mask and not, as he believes,
from the world. The mask has been his excuse to become
Pan — the compensation of self-pity rather than the real

suffering of maturity. And with Brown, in his turn, it becomes the same. The laughter born of such suffering can not have the ring of eternity — nor bring the ultimate peace of the poet's quest.

XVIII

"LAZARUS LAUGHED"

Thus Laughed Zarathustra

"LAZARUS LAUGHED" is one of the O'Neill plays almost unknown to theatre-going audiences. It presents enormous production difficulties, not only because of a very large cast and a great complexity of masking and costuming, but chiefly because the idea of the titanic laughter of Lazarus is almost impossible to translate into theatrical terms without losing most of its majesty. The play has actually been produced upon the Pacific Coast, but to most followers of O'Neill's work, it is known only in its published form. In that form, however, it remains one of his major poetical works, and of immeasurable importance to the sequence of his plays.

The inner connection between "The Great God Brown" and "Lazarus Laughed" is immediate and direct. Lazarus is Brown — Man, if you will — brought back from death, and from the discovery made in Brown's dying words that the "laughter of Heaven sows earth with a rain of tears" and that from "earth's transfigured birth-pain the laughter of Man returns" to bless God. In Miriam, the wife of Lazarus, we find a union of Cybel, as the symbol of mother earth, and of Margaret. Her mask, which covers only the upper part of her face, "is the pure pallor of marble, the expression that of a statue of Woman, of her eternal acceptance of the compulsion of motherhood, the inevitable cycle of love into pain into joy and new love into separation and pain again and the loneliness of age." These words are almost the counterpart of the closing words of Cybel, who, standing above the dead Brown, cries out : "Always spring comes again bearing life ! . . . Spring again ! — life again ! — summer and fall and death and peace again ! — but always, always, love and conception and birth and pain again — spring bearing the intolerable chalice of life again ! — bearing the glorious, blazing crown of life again !" This is the figure of woman growing into the maturity of acceptance — no longer the child to be carried to the gates of Heaven in play. But O'Neill adds also the picture of Margaret brooding over the child, the Pan, under her heart, when he writes : "The eyes of the mask are almost closed. Their gaze turns within, oblivious to the life outside, as they dream down on the child forever in memory at her breast." Then, beneath the mask, there is the figure of a third woman rumored, one whose mouth "is sensitive and sad, tender with an eager, understanding smile of self-forgetful love, the lips still fresh and young." In this third woman it seems as if we have once more the mature tenderness of Maria de Cordova and of Beatriz, her emissary.

But it is Lazarus, "freed now from the fear of death" and wearing no mask, who utterly dominates the scene. He is "tall and powerful, about fifty years of age, with a mass of gray-black hair and a heavy beard. His face recalls that of a statue of a divinity of Ancient Greece in its general structure and particularly in its quality of detached serenity. It is dark-complected, ruddy and brown, the color of rich earth upturned by the plow, calm but furrowed deep with the marks of former suffering endured with a grim fortitude that had never softened into resignation." This Lazarus, then, is more than a suffering Brown and Anthony brought back from death. There is something of the hardness of Ephraim Cabot in him as well — of the humanity that hardens itself into an identification with the stern father God of the Old Testament as understood in Puritan tradition. His pride is as yet untamed, in spite of the revelation he has received. The alliance of pride and self-pity is fully apparent — the same alliance that made Dion Anthony and Bill Brown discover most of their sufferings in their masks rather than in realities.

From those who are watching Lazarus in awe, we find even more connections with the poet's past. "Of late years his life had been one long misfortune. One after another his children died" — the children in earlier plays who could not live. "They were all girls. Lazarus had

no luck." "The last was a boy, the one that died at
birth. You are forgetting him." Is this the child of
Eben and Abbie? Are the others the frail ghosts of
Robert Mayo's dead daughter and of the children of
Curtis and Martha Jayson? "Not only did his son die
but Miriam could never bear him more children." These
are but a few of the many echoes of the past that seem to
crowd over the first few pages of "Lazarus Laughed" —
the sorrow of the Man who can not Create. There is
even a direct memory of poor Robert Mayo in this comment of another bystander : "But he could not blame
bad luck for everything. Take the loss of his father's
wealth since he took over the management. That was his
own doing. He was a bad farmer, a poor breeder of
sheep, and a bargainer so easy to cheat it hurt one's conscience to trade with him." Lazarus is indeed many men
in one.

And then we learn that after the miracle, as Jesus went
His way, "Lazarus, looking after Him, began to laugh
softly like a man in love with God!" When Lazarus
himself first speaks to the throng, in a voice "that is like
a loving whisper of hope and confidence" it is to tell them
that "There is no death!" When they press him for
some word from "beyond," he at last says "in a voice of
loving exaltation," that "There is only life! I heard
the heart of Jesus laughing in my heart ; 'There is Eternal Life in No,' it said, 'and there is the same Eternal
Life in Yes! Death is the fear between!' And my

heart reborn to love of life cried 'Yes !' and I laughed in
the laughter of God !" And then he "begins to laugh,
softly at first — a laugh so full of a complete acceptance
of life, a profound assertion of joy in living, so devoid of
all self-consciousness or fear, that it is like a great bird
song triumphant in depths of sky, proud and powerful,
infectious with love, casting on the listener an enthralling
spell."

To one who has lived with the poet so far in imagination, and accompanied him on every stage of his painful
pilgrimage, it would be an unbounded joy to accept this
laughter of Lazarus as the ultimate discovery of unity
and peace — as the true laughter of the love of God.
But it is "proud" as well as powerful. It is too heart-
breakingly reminiscent — though on a far higher plane —
of the proud laughter of Brutus Jones, too suddenly
released from pain and inferiority. It shoots to depths
of sky too swiftly, too triumphantly, too pitifully like a
"great bird song" — which is mortal and destined to fall
back to earth or into the embracing sea. "Laugh !
Laugh with me !" cries Lazarus "on a final note of compelling exultation" and again he cries, "Death is dead !
Fear is no more ! There is only life ! There is only
laughter !" And the great crowd, all but Miriam who
watches him with tenderness, laughs with him and takes
up his cry, "Fear is no more ! There is no death !
There is only life ! There is only laughter !" There is
no peace in such laughter, no true serenity, for there is

none of the humility in it that brings life to the creature
and makes him share in the laughter of the Creator.   It
is thus that Zarathustra might have laughed.

It is difficult, perhaps, in catching the true spirit of this
laughter of Lazarus, to establish a common ground of
feeling between listeners.   The partly historical setting,
the basis of Christ's miracle, and the connotations of
Lazarus' words are apt to place the whole question within
a particular sphere of religious judgment or appraisal.
Yet it is possible to find equivalent terms within universal
experience — within the sphere, so to speak, of natural
religion and the natural experience of the human spirit.
If we take man only in his relation to nature, we find him
most at peace when he accepts and works with the great
and mysterious powers operating in and around him.
This true humility is no more than an acceptance of something greater and more powerful than himself.   It need
not be and should not be a slavish fear, but rather fear
in the more profound sense of deep and abiding respect,
the respect of a necessary partnership and dependence in
both being and achievement.   Nor should it be a sense
of exaggerated self-abasement, as ancient peasants before
the lightning, but rather a passion of the creative intellect,
as if to make the lightning harmless by setting up a
lightning rod of the soul.   There is peace in such a
dependent partnership of man and nature, but not pride —
a note of full-hearted thanksgiving rather than of a
triumphant bird song — of calmness rather than exulta-

tion — of deep joy in something shared rather than of superiority as in something bestowed.

In some such terms as these, as well as in terms of God the Creator and Man the Creature, we can sense the portents of disaster in the proud Superman laughter of Lazarus. The first notes of that laughter — "like a man in love with God" — were different. But that was after the first touch of the miracle. It is the change in the laughter — as of one released and then forgetting his rescuer — which brings the note of pride and of self-sufficiency. It is as if Lazarus, admitted to the secret of God's laughter, suddenly felt himself a god, a bestower instead of a receiver, the player of a great instrument of understanding rather than the instrument itself.

Perhaps the poet himself felt this — for the laughter of Lazarus does not bring peace to men, as the perfection of a saint might bring peace and beauty to those about him. It brings instead the wild adulation of the mob, an hysteria not unlike a Bacchic orgy, a desire to make Lazarus himself a divinity, and the death of those dearest to Lazarus, including at length Miriam herself, who grows old as Lazarus grows ever younger. Exaltedly, Lazarus cries out : "The greatness of Saviors is that they may not save ! The greatness of Man is that no god can save him — until he becomes a god !" And later he says in a voice of infinite disdain, "Sometimes it is hard to laugh — even *at* men !" In the poet's concept, he becomes, little by little, not an incarnation of love but of solitary, almost contemptuous pride, not one who sorrows for men because they are deaf and will not hear, but one who disdains men for not hearing and for forgetting, oblivious by now of the fact that a revelation was granted to him, and that without that revelation he, too, would have remained both blind and deaf. In the end, there is not even one person to whom Lazarus is able to communicate the truth he believes he has discovered. Many are infected by his presence, but no one lives to carry on his message. Pride has choked the seed of his words.

After the crucifixion of Christ, the Emperor Tiberius sends his soldiers to summon Lazarus to Rome. Caligula, the heir of Tiberius, meets him at Athens. By this time Lazarus has changed until "his countenance now might well be that of the positive masculine Dionysius, closest to the soil of the Grecian gods, a Son of Man, born of a mortal. Not the coarse, drunken Dionysius, nor the effeminate god, but Dionysius in his middle period, more comprehensive in his symbolism, the soul of the recurring seasons, of living and dying as processes in eternal growth, of the wine of life stirring forever in the sap and blood and loam of things." It is this being who wins both the love and the hate of Caligula — the man to whom death and cruelty have been means to rule the world, who loves to kill because he himself fears death, who battens on the fears of men that he may forget his own fear. He is a symbol of the Rome whose "will is so sick that it must kill in order to be aware of life at all." He loves Lazarus because of the secret he would like to share with him and hopes to discover ; he hates him because he knows in his heart that he will never discover the secret.   And Miriam, growing constantly older, and fearing Rome — the spirit of Caligula — suddenly pleads with Lazarus :   "I begin to know the torture of the fear of death, Lazarus — not of my death but of yours — not of the passing of your man's body but of the going away from me of your laughter which is to me as my son, my little boy !"   Here, then, we have revealed at last the true nature of the proud laughter of Lazarus and of the "other self" in Caligula. His laughter is the "little boy" guarded in the breast of the woman — the mask of Dionysius, hidden under the heart of Margaret, living again proudly, as Margaret promised it would — and Caligula the envious mask of Billy Brown, ready to strike Dion or to draw strength from him.   Though Lazarus is unmasked, the poet himself is wearing the mask of Lazarus as a proud defiance of fear and death, laughing with the voice of Pan, forgetting the miracle that once made him laugh "as if he were in love with God."   The irony is terrific — and beneath the mask, we can only try to imagine the suffering of the poet's soul — an Anthony imprisoned in the laughter of a child, held under the heart of a woman who mistakes the laughter for the man !

As if to confirm this concealed spirit of regression, we have the ever-increasing youth of Lazarus.   He is literally and figuratively moving back to childhood, with his

wife becoming older and older — more like his mother.
His torture in the flames at the hands of Tiberius and his
death at the hands of Caligula come before he has passed
back beyond the stage of young manhood. Caligula, the
beast, kills him, as the gorilla killed the Hairy Ape, and
for the same reason in an opposite extreme. The Hairy
Ape sank too low in striving to "belong." Lazarus soars
too high — and the highest beast, Caligula, now Caesar,
because he has murdered Tiberius, kills him. Lazarus
does not "belong" among men because he has exalted
himself to the position of a god.

The conscious intention of the poet was possibly very
different from this. The play is written in a mood of
tremendous exaltation, starting with the great conception
of death as the beginning of eternal life and laughter
with God. But the unconscious mood quickly passes
beyond this to the pride aroused by discovery — pride
that leads to a denial of death rather than an affirmation
of death as birth to a greater life. It is not in the love of
God, something greater than himself, that Lazarus
preaches the death of death, but in love of life, in man's
love of a god in himself. Thus the regression of the
incest theme is continued in its subtlest form of self-
worship and the death dealing pride which that worship
nourishes. In permitting the poisoning of Miriam by
Pompeia, the wife of Tiberius, in permitting the death
and joyous self-destruction of his followers, Lazarus is
taking to himself the prerogatives of God-head, of the

bestower of life, sanctioning that which only the Giver of life may sanction, because He is taking life back to Himself. This would be the religious interpretation of the pride of Lazarus, but it would be equally discernible in a naturalistic interpretation as the insubordination of Man against Life, under the mask of an affirmation of life, man defying the lightning. It is a heartbreaking realization when one knows the length and intensity of the poet's struggle for true freedom, but one which the soul of the poet was soon to understand and record in that multiple drama of a single soul in bewilderment — "Strange Interlude." Before that play begins, the joyous, life-loving Gordon, an aviator, soaring in the skies like the defiant spirit of Lazarus, is brought down in flames — even as Lazarus was burned to dust !

XIX

"STRANGE INTERLUDE"

Surface Without Soul

"OH, Gordon, my dear one ! . . . oh, spirit so brave and generous and gay ! . . . ashes dissolving into mud ! . . . mud and ashes ! . . . that's all ! . . . gone ! . . . gone forever from me !" Thus Nina Leeds, the heroine of "Strange Inter lude," speaks to the departed spirit of Gordon, the aviator whom she loved, who was brought down in flames in the war. The words are in one of those many "asides" by which O'Neill sought to express for the audience the inner thoughts and emotions of his characters, so often at complete variance with their spoken words. The technique is a variation on the use of the mask, although essentially the same in spirit, a contrasting of the inner man with his outer attitude toward the world. The heart of Nina Leeds is with the god-like creature, the modern Lazarus, killed in the flames kindled by the Caligula-like cruelty and greed of man in war.

In a multiple sense, this play is in fact as well as in title a strange interlude for the poet's harassed soul. It is an interlude of scrupulous self-examination. No other play of O'Neill's is so consciously and deliberately and even ferociously self-analytical. The very method used, of the asides, is a symptom of this irresistible desire to pull apart and dissect every phrase, every superficial attitude, every apparently spontaneous action, and to discover the truth beneath it. But few such conscious efforts are wholly successful. In "Strange Interlude" there is an extraordinary mixture of the explained and the unexplained, of conscious self-examination and of unconscious self-revelation, of appraisal of the past and the present and of instinctive prophecy of the future. It is important, for example, that for the first time since "Anna Christie" and "Diff'rent" the character of a woman is distinctly the dominating dramatic figure. The feminine aspect of the poet's soul has been growing in strength and inner significance. It is no longer the child of "All God's Chillun," nor the frail maidenhood of Kukachin. It has become more insistently like the faint memory of Maria de Cordova or the more recent memory of Miriam. Yet it is more than an echo of the past. It is woman in all her primitive aspects — tender, reckless, defiant, protective and absorbing, possessive and creative and proudly untamed. Abbie, in "Desire Under the Elms," was the object of masculine desire. In "Strange Interlude," Nina Leeds is the one who desires. But it is defensive desire always — desire for everything except that which might touch the inner shrine dedicated to the dead Gordon — desire for the surface of the earth, thwarted by a fear of seeking its heart. It is as if the poet's soul turned back in fear from the overwhelming introversion of "Desire Under the Elms," of "Great God Brown" and of "Lazarus," and sought, through the feminine side, to build up the outer and surface self.

This is a common enough human experience. After the first battles of the many selves, and the first false hopes of conquest, comes the great settling back into the inner depths, a mood of regression seeking solace in the dead but tenderly remembered days of immaturity. But those memories are, for the moment, enemies. They do not bring the peace to manhood that they once brought to childhood. There is a sense almost of guilt in going back to them — like the boy who runs from a street fight to his mother's arms, and then feels ashamed of himself. No peace is found in escape, or in the momentary false pride of escape. The spirit of youth must turn forward again and be willing to face the street fights of its spiritual life. This brings the strange interlude of the soul — the examination of admitted weaknesses, the sense of rage with one's own cowardice and inadequacy, and the passionate desire to compensate by an outer "hardening." Shyness must be overcome by building up a bold exterior, by taking possession of the concrete masculine qualities that are needed in the world of men ; and, curiously enough, it is often the feminine quality, the feminine instinct for possessing the concrete, that is used in acquiring these outer masculine qualities. In the language of commonest experience, marriage has made a man of many a boy. In the language of poets, using the feminine instinct of the soul has often brought maturity for the first time — that fullness of soul which brings peace, the very thing which O'Neill's Marco Polo refused to accept.

The danger, of course, is the unbalanced use of the feminine quality — its use merely to accept the hard, outer qualities of manhood. There is apt to be too much fear left of the maternal feminine, to which the spirit has so recently regressed in false hope. By contrast, outer values assume an exaggerated importance. The search for them becomes too ferocious and untamed — and ends by defeating itself. This is largely what happens in "Strange Interlude," and the full import of the story to the poet's spiritual progress can only be understood when this is kept clearly in mind at every point of the play.

There are nine important characters in "Strange Interlude" — eight of them in the play itself, and the dead Gordon making the important ninth. There is Professor Leeds, Nina's father, who, prompted by a half-admitted sinister jealousy, prevented Gordon from marrying Nina before he left for the war. Like so many other parental characters in the O'Neill plays, he represents the interference of outworn external authority in the development of the new individual soul. It is not Gordon's death so much as the fact that they were never united before his death that leaves the incurable wound in Nina's spirit — that same denial and prevention of creation which under-

lies so many of the earlier plays. Then there is Charles
Marsden, the writer, inexorably bound to the protecting
arms of his mother, afraid of life, inhibited in every true
creative instinct, taking out in words and stories everything that he is afraid to tackle in life itself. He loves
Nina, but to her he is "dear old Charlie," or "uncle
Charlie"; after Professor Leeds' death he actually becomes, in her mind, "father Charlie." He represents the
first of the three male principles which Nina seeks to
possess to cover up the void left by Gordon. Edmund
Darrell is the wholly male scientist, a doctor, a man of
strong passions held under iron discipline of devotion to
his work. The third man is Sam Evans, a classmate of
Gordon's, an awkward young colt in the earlier scenes of
the play, but of the kind "likely to make his way" in an
eminently practical world of advertising and business—
the complete extravert. When Nina, without enthusiasm,
thinks of marrying him, she can only say: "Sam is a
nice boy. Yes, it would be a career for me to bring a
career to his surface. I would be busy—surface life—
no more depths, please God!" As it turns out, Nina's
whole life is devoted to nothing more than building up
this amiable surface extravert—the overcompensation
from her fear of the depths represented by the dead
Gordon, with whom she was prevented from achieving
true creation.

The other character of the first part of the play is Mrs.
Evans, Sam's mother—and upon her the poet lays the

burden of revealing to Nina, after her child by Sam has actually been conceived, that there is incurable insanity in the family. Again a parental character obstructs the course of nature by implanting a fear of life. It is she who insists that Nina do away with her child before it is born — to protect Sam! Mrs. Evans has tried to protect Sam zealously by not telling him of the family curse, hoping that through ignorance of it he would never experience the fear of insanity that might bring it on — as it did with her own husband. Now she puts the whole burden of Sam's future upon Nina. She must save him from his father's fate — be satisfied to have no children — protect him to make up for her responsibility in having married him without love. She never admits nor suggests the possibility that nature, with a further diluting of the Evans blood, might bring a cure. She lives in a spirit of fear and denial. Nina must share the horror she herself faced. Her sinister counsel prevails, and Nina has the life within her destroyed — for the sake of Sam, the man of "surface."

But this new denial of life proves too much, and defeats itself. Sam begins to blame himself for having no children. The sense of defeat preys on his mind and imperils his success. Nina, now devoted wholly to building up this surface male, decides that she must have a child by another man — for Sam's sake — and let him believe it is his own. For this purpose, she selects Dr. Darrell as the father. She tells him the whole story, and puts the blame for her marriage up to him, because he had suggested and encouraged it, and had failed, professionally, to find out the truth about the Evans family in advance. She feels a sense of guilt—admits that it would be adultery—and yet forces Darrell, bit by bit, to encourage her in the name of science and of happiness for her husband! It must be done without love. "I should be so humbly grateful" she tells him, and Darrell, fighting between his love for her and his "scientific" reasoning that it would be the right thing to do, consents. Thus, not only is real life and real creation destroyed for the sake of the surface Sam, but he is to be given a false life to live on, one that is not his—a surface image to fatten the pride of the surface man, and an image created in sin.

The sin, of course, reveals the truth to Nina, that she really loves Ned Darrell, and has loved him all along. For a time, her resolution to help Sam gives way, and she tries to persuade Darrell to be first her lover, and then her husband when she can divorce Sam. But Darrell himself prevents this by abruptly breaking the news to Sam of his prospective "fatherhood," and then leaving for Europe. Nina at last decides to go through with her original plan of sacrificing all her desires to the extraverted Sam. The feminine intuition of Charlie Marsden, whose mother has recently died, suspects the truth of what is happening. But he can not tear himself away from Nina's side. Nina is now in a position to keep all her three men in her spiritual possession—Sam as her husband, Darrell as the male she loves in place of Gordon, but will henceforth possess only in the negative sense of holding his love at a distance, and Marsden as the easy symbol of her father and as a devoted, never exacting and forgiving friend. Their lives are hers to make or ruin, but Sam is to be the sole beneficiary of the double sin against life. Small wonder that Nina keeps crying out that "God is a mother." She, as the feminine side of the soul has tried to usurp the place of the creator — to select and choose who shall live and who shall be the source of whatever life is permitted to live. Here we have, in the sweep of the poet's imagination, the extraordinary over-compensation in the use of the feminine side to build up the male masks with which to meet surface life.

Sam, under the stimulus of parenthood, which he also feels as a proof of Nina's love, begins to succeed in business and to gain in confidence and assurance. Nina acquires a certain respect for him, colored by the fact that his surface personality makes no demands on her. "Thank God for Sammy!" she exclaims in an aside, "I know he's mine . . . no jealousy . . . no fear . . . no pain . . . I've found peace . . ." Their son, named for the dead Gordon, becomes the fourth male in Nina's life. In a curious way, she feels him to be the son of all three men, and this thought gives her possessive soul its transient peace. But when Darrell returns from Europe, unable to stay away from her, the assumed perfection of her scheme begins to break down. He wants her for himself and wants their son. But she will give up neither her son nor Sam. She makes Darrell consent to the ignominious idea of becoming her lover, and is doomed from then on to watch his gradual disintegration before her eyes. Sam, the weakling, becomes stronger and stronger as Darrell grows weaker and weaker. Little Gordon loves his supposed father more and more every day and resents Darrell more and more bitterly. After a few years, Darrell spends only short intervals with Nina and the rest of his time at some far off tropical health station. Marsden, whom Nina begins to look upon as the ideal companion for one's old age, becomes the understanding one, making fewer and fewer demands upon her. Little Gordon, who has heard of the exploits of his mother's first love, becomes ambitious to be like the original Gordon, so that he can supplant all others in his mother's affection.

In all these developments, through the use of the "asides," the poet is severely self-analytical. But what is implied is even more important than what is expressed — that the spirit of "Lazarus," after dying one death in flames, has continued his progress in becoming more youthful until he has actually become a child again, to be held in his mother's arms — a child born of the feminine principle of the soul, but fathered partly by Marsden, the embodiment of the fear of life and its inferiorities (the spirit of poor Jim Harris of "All God's Chillun"), partly by the surface man of action who was once so weak and without a soul (the spirit of Marco Polo, perhaps) and partly by the aggressive male, once strong, but growing weaker now as the woman uses his strength to build up the weakling.   In Darrell, we have the reincarnation of those harder, tougher spirits found in most of the earlier plays.   Yet this new child of the soul, although strong in body, is born under a cloud of cheating and lying and a denial of faith in life.   One feels that he, too, is born to die in flames, like Gordon — and in the poet's next play, "Dynamo," that is exactly what happens.   Reuben Light is killed in the flames of a terrific short circuit in the dynamo he has made his new "female" god!

The closing parts of "Strange Interlude" carry forward to the period of the new Gordon's young manhood.   He rows in a winning crew race, and Sam, who has acquired high blood pressure along with success, has a stroke from the excitement.   Just prior to this, Nina has tried to break up the engagement of Gordon to a young girl who somewhat resembles Nina in her own youth.   But Ned Darrell, who has now regained his strength in the final death of his love for Nina, interferes and prevents her telling the young girl the same story Sam's mother had told Nina.   Darrell at last understands her maniacal possessiveness and openly accuses her of having tried to play God and interfere too much with human lives.   When Sam is stricken, Nina at last realizes that she must once more make a sacrifice for his sake, and resolves to give Gordon to the girl he loves.

A few months later, when Sam has died, both Nina and Darrell understand that this event, which they had secretly hoped for and waited for in their youth, has come too late. Their love is dead. Only memories remain. But with the memories, there is also Charlie Marsden. He is now wholly "father" Marsden to Nina, who, in her declining years, having passed beyond desire, is only too glad to settle down with him in a marriage of fading days and the peace of exhaustion. As they are quietly in each other's arms, an airplane overhead carries Gordon and the girl he loves to their wedding. Nina cries out to them "Fly up to heaven, Gordon! Fly with your love to heaven! Fly always! Never crash to earth like my old Gordon! Be happy, dear! You've got to be happy!" Then she turns to Charlie. "Gordon is dead, Father," she says, "I've just had a cable. What I mean is, he flew away to another life — my son, Gordon, Charlie. So we're alone again — just as we used to be."

Perhaps if there were real renunciation in Nina's farewell to Gordon, if her giving up of him were for his own sake, and not a last gift to Sam, the man of surface, and if her final peace were not the involved peace of a return to Charlie, the one who makes no demands, but rather the peace of sacrifice, there would be more spirit of hope, more rumor of ultimate victory in this tortured, arrogant, possessive and bitterly self-accusing play. But as a story in which all the deeper realities are sacrificed to build up lies and false values and things of the surface, its ultimate

peace seems as false as the pride of the laughter of
Lazarus.   It is as if the poet turned first to the male
instincts in his soul and found there a pride ready to
become a god, and then turned to the feminine instinct,
only to find it, too, eager to become a mother god — each
seeking in its own way to shape and determine life rather
than to accept life and work with it humbly and in peace,
to gain all by surrendering all.   Pride and lust fuse and
become one in this twisted struggle to escape from the terrors of regression.   The only humility is the debased
humility of Charlie, self-condemning and impotent.   Nowhere can be found the true and positive humility of
self-respect under a power greater than self.   But above
all, there is the false throwing of all life's desires and
powers to the meaningless surface — the boy rushing back
from the shame of his mother's protection to finish the
street fight, as if in that alone he could reinstate his manhood, or, in the deeper sense of the poet's language, as if
maturity could be found only in the mask of life.   The
overwhelming truths and discoveries of "The Great God
Brown" seem to be forgotten.   The pride in those discoveries was too great and blotted out the vision of them.
Beyond their crest, the poet's soul has found another dark
valley — like Dante at the entrance to the Inferno, "a
darkened way, where the direct path is lost to sight"—
"una via oscura, che la diritta via era smarita."

XX

"DYNAMO"

Center Without Surface

FROM the surface to the center !   It was a strange interlude indeed for the soul of a poet, driven by inner neces-
sity toward creation, to rest, even for a short time, in the
love of surface things, to sacrifice every inner value to
externals.   Yet we have seen that even in this sudden
passion to harden the surface, the forces of regression still
held sway.   The spirit of Gordon and of Lazarus found
itself again within the mother, to be fathered this time by
science in the symbol of Darrell and to grow as a living
lie, as the son of the surface man.   In this vast confusion,
this mingling of surface pride and regressive desires, one
could not hope to discover anything but the seed of
further tragedy.   In "Dynamo," the poet's bewildered
spirit, in the person of Reuben Light, turns back swiftly
and ferociously from the surface to the center and there
finds death in the flames — the second Gordon crashing to
earth.

"Dynamo" is a play of frenzy.   It is as much a denial
of the whole of life — of the harmonious balance between

the interior and the exterior life — as "Strange Interlude," but in opposite terms. It is the complete sacrifice of the external realities and obligations, just as "Strange Interlude" was the complete sacrifice of the interior truth. The mystics have discovered ultimately that as men, living in finite terms, that is, in space and time, the secret of inner peace lies in building up the strength of both the inner and the outer life, and in animating the strength of the finite outer life with the power and truth of the interior life, that which reaches toward the infinite center of all things, toward God. To seek to withdraw entirely from outer realities is to deny one's present finite nature, to become, as it were, a spiritual glutton. To seek only outer realities is to become a material glutton. Either way lies destruction — that "in-sanity" which throws the creature of body and spirit into a frenzy of hopeless denial and blackness. In essence, the quest for harmony of the interior and the exterior life is the problem faced by the two "brothers" in "Beyond the Horizon," and remotely or directly in nearly every succeeding play of O'Neill's. The plays of regression, including those which use the symbol of the incest theme, are those which seek escape from all outer realities. The plays of material possessiveness are those which seek to deny the interior man. In both cases, there is a denial of creation. The interior and the exterior must be united to create, to feel that eternal pulsing rhythm of the universe in which matter is animated by spirit, in which the center bestows life upon the periphery, in which God enters the lives of created Men.

In "Dynamo," the conflicting forces of inner and outer man are represented in two families, living as neighbors — a minister and his wife and son, and an atheist and his wife and daughter. The minister, Hutchins Light, is the embodiment of that familiar figure of the stern father god of Puritan tradition — a tradition which, through ignoring the maternal symbol of the Mother of God, hardened itself in a single finite male attitude and lost, not only tenderness, but also all that balance in symbols through which finite man might hope, even faintly, to catch the vision of infinite Unity. The minister's wife is by nature a materialist, though dutifully following in externals the beliefs of her husband. Their son, Reuben, lives in fear of his father and in the protecting love of his mother, his own religious beliefs being a composite reflection of theirs, an acceptance of fear and an unquestioning faith in maternal protection. When the mother, stirred by jealousy of his love of their neighbor's daughter, betrays him to the father, he loses all faith — very much as Dion Anthony lost faith when Billy Brown, at the age of four, struck him through envy.

The neighbor, Ramsay Fife, is a scoffing and aggressive atheist, a fully hardened materialist. But his cow-like wife, in contrast, is a sentimental moon-dreamer, a symbol of earthy motherhood seeking something mystical in the skies or in the mysterious whir of the dynamos which her husband operates as superintendent of the hydro-electric plant. Their daughter, Ada, is a cross between them both, accepting, in dutiful ignorance, her father's materialism and, by instinct, her mother's earthiness. To Reuben Light, she becomes the object of external desires, the symbol of external life to be won and mastered. But while he is dominated by fear of his father and trust in his mother, he is timid and shy before Ada's sensuality.

In his mother's betrayal of him to his father (who feels that the boy's love of Ada is a damning of his soul through association with the atheist's family) Reuben finds the impulse to break the bond of fear, and delivers himself over to the hard externals. He leaves home and toughens himself by jobs picked up on his travels. He boasts that he has electrocuted his father's God, and sends his mother messages, telling her this, and asking her not to be a fool. A year or more later, when he returns, he is a different man, cold, calculating, aggressive in his earthly desires, except for his yearning to see his mother again. But he finds that she has died, and in her dying breath has repeated to his father the admonition not to be a fool. Reuben feels exalted, as if he had made a convert to his new god of electricity — but the yearning for his mother becomes more intense than ever.

Almost cynically, he takes Ada's love, and finds it easy to obtain. He proudly discards all idea that he has committed a sin. He feels himself free from old "superstitions." But he does go to his mother's grave, and there the yearning comes over him to talk to her. "I'd like to reach her somehow," he says to himself, "no one knows what happens after death — even science doesn't — there may be some kind of hereafter." Then, later, "Funny, that hunch I got when I was talking to Ada . . . about praying to electricity, if you knew how . . . it was like a message . . . Mother believed what I believed when she died . . . maybe it came from her . . . Aw, that's superstitious junk . . . but why is it ? . . . look at how mysterious all this electrical wave stuff is in radio and everything . . . that's scientific fact . . . and why couldn't something like that that no one understands yet ? . . . between the dead and the living ?"

Slowly this thought becomes an obsession with him, this notion that in the mysterious powers of the dynamo there is something god-like, something like the love of a mother —"a great, dark mother ! . . . that's what the dynamo is ! . . . that's what life is !" He listens to the humming song of the machine. "If you could only get back into that . . . know what it means . . . then you'd know the real God !" Then, in secret, he prays to the dynamo. "Oh, Mother of Life, my mother is dead, she has passed back into you, tell her to forgive me, and to help me find your truth !" As if in reflection of the boastful age of science in which he lived, the poet calls upon the man-made machine to give him the secret of the maternity of nature and to answer the yearning of his soul, which has denied God.

As the months go on, the obsession becomes more and more dominant. Reuben wants to give up the love of Ada, as if it made him impure in the sight of his new mother image, the dynamo. He finds a sympathetic ear in the earthy and sentimental Mrs. Fife. He pours out to her, as if she had taken his mother's place among the living, his passion for the new mother-god. "Like some one singing me to sleep," he exclaims, "my mother — when I was a kid — calling me back to somewhere far off where I'd been once long ago and known peace!" Thus, in spite of his surface hardening, it is the regressive call, the summons back to childhood, which is stronger than reality, stronger than his love for Ada, whom he thinks of as a girl, not as a woman, a mother. The old possessing spirit of the sea comes back to him, too. "It's the sea rising up in clouds, falling on the earth in rain, made that river that drives the turbines that drive Dynamo! The sea makes her heart beat, too!" As his frenzy and madness increase, he begins to deify this new goddess, and to want to sacrifice to her all earthly desires. "She wants some one man to love her purely and when she finds him worthy she will love him and give him the secret of truth and he will become the new saviour who will bring happiness and peace to men." The dynamo and his mother's spirit become fused in one great image, summoning him to return, to leave Ada and reality.

But Ada comes to him one night as he is passionately waiting for the miracle of a revelation from the spirit of the dynamo. Her physical presence is too much for him. He yields again to his love for her — and then feels that he has made himself impure, that he has betrayed the thing that would have made him worthy of his dynamo-mother image. He kills Ada, calling her a harlot, as his own mother had once done, and then rushes to the dynamo, seizing the great brushes until the current short circuits through his body and kills him in a blaze of blue light. As he dies, his voice "rises in a moan that is a mingling of pain and loving consummation, and this cry dies into a sound that is like the crooning of a baby and merges and is lost in the dynamo's hum."

In no other play, except possibly "Desire Under the Elms," has the imagination of the poet yielded so completely to the regressive call back to childhood. Again he has tried to kill the feminine side — Ada — through whom he might have achieved the creative function of life, and has sought death and oblivion in the "crooning of a baby" in the arms of the mother god. He seems to catch the very spirit of an age which, in the pride of its discoveries in science, made science a new god for the destruction of life itself — an age that destroyed itself by short-circuiting God, by attempting to live only in the surface and then, as in a tremendous revulsion, by seeking oblivion in the secrets of mother nature and in the negation of the outer realities, of the demand for adjustment of man to man, of nation to nation, of mankind to life itself under the animating spirit of God.

The frenzied spirit of "Dynamo" is a cry of utter exhaustion, as if the interminable strain upon the poet's driving will had become almost too great to bear. Yet there is a gleam of hope in its very brutality and directness. All pretence seems to be abandoned, all the polite symbols of masks and masked attitudes. The spirit of the growing man, driven frantic by the blows of outer life and by the gad-flies of circumstance, cries out "Mother." But it is not until this man is ready to make another woman the mother of his own seed, to become a father to the children of his own spirit, and to live humbly and strongly in a world of both inner and outer realities that he will find peace at last, the ultimate fulfillment of that obligation to create in the image of the Creator which is the task of man in every generation of the spirit and the flesh.

XXI

"MOURNING BECOMES ELECTRA"

Death of the Old Gods

THE fates and furies of Greek tragedy, of the incestuous curse of the House of Atreus, at last take full possession of the imagination of the poet after the terrifying, unmasked confession of "Dynamo." There is no more place now for concealment of that temptation of the soul that lies deeper than regression itself, although part of it — the temptation of Lucifer which ended in the primal sin, self-worship. "Mourning Becomes Electra" is the drama of a soul at mortal grips with the love of self, the deadly poison of the spirit that denies all creation because it would be self-creating, self-sufficient, both creator and creature, man co equal with God.

The House of Mannon in this play is the summation of Man, as the poet has come to know him, in which the multitudinous characters that have gone before are only pale, premonitory shadows of the realities at last revealed — the false prides, the timid abasements, the yearning for childlike peace, the struggles for freedom, the exultant discoveries and crests of hope and the heartrending plunges into renewed darkness. Each of these Men of Mannon must die if the soul is to live, killed by themselves, dying to their old selves in the mystic formula of the poets and saints, if they are to be reborn to life and love. In this struggle to the death, it is only the spirit of the woman which lives on in solitary expiation, "until the curse is paid out and the last Mannon is let die." Behind the closed doors of that house, the feminine soul, last to die to itself, must find the secret of purgation in silence and alone, beyond the gaze of men, in the sanctuary of the immortal inner will, where only the breath of God may touch its darkness.

In outer form, "Mourning Becomes Electra" follows in a reasonably close modern parallel the tragedy of the House of Atreus, but the fates and furies of the Greek tragedy become the inner subjective desires, passions and perversities of the Mannon household. In laying the scene in New England, just after the Civil War, O'Neill carried the parallel still further, for it is in New England that one finds many of the symbols of Greek civilization. One discovers the similarities of a strongly developed feeling for homestead and family continuity, a conspicuous outward order and symmetry and an attitude of repression which may be held to cover an inner chaos of emotions ready to explode at times with extraordinary violence, a co-existence of mental detachment and serenity with emotional upheaval, the calmness of a Socrates with the turmoil of an Æschylus or a Euripides, a mental Utopia living with an emotional House of Atreus.]

O'Neill's Electra is really a trilogy, three plays or stages in the climax of the house of Mannon. The first is called "Homecoming"; the second, "The Hunted"; and the third, "The Haunted." In the first play, General Ezra Mannon, one of a long line whose wealth and position have been gathered from the sea, returns from the war at a time when his partly foreign wife, Christine, has secretly been giving her love to a sea captain, Adam Brant. She knows him to be the son of another Mannon who "disgraced" his family by marrying a French-Canadian servant girl. Brant is genuinely in love with Christine, but in first seeking her out, his sole purpose was revenge on the present head of the house of Mannon. Christine's daughter, Lavinia (the Electra of the story) is devoted to her father with an almost fanatical attachment, and doubly resents her mother's infidelity, partly because she herself is attracted to Brant, who resembles her father, and partly because she has always instinctively taken her father's part against her mother, whom she hates and of whom she is inwardly jealous.

In the first play, Lavinia's brother, Orin Mannon (the Orestes of the tragedy) is still away in camp, recovering from a serious head wound which has weakened his whole nervous system. But we learn that Orin is as much devoted to his mother, of whom he constantly dreams in his illness, as Lavinia is devoted to her father. Yet between brother and sister there is a similar bond of deep attachment — part of that sinister cloud of love-of-self, as reflected in one's own family, which hovers over the ill-fated house.) Lavinia lets her mother know that she has discovered her infidelity, but instead of threatening to tell her father, offers to keep silent if her mother will send Brant away forever. Christine is quick to strike at the truth of Lavinia's action. "You wanted Adam Brant for yourself," she says accusingly, "And now you know you can't have him, you're determined that at least you'll take him from me ! . . . But if you told your father, I'd have to go away with Adam. He'd be mine still. You can't bear that thought, even at the price of my disgrace, can you ? . . . I know you, Vinnie ! I've watched you ever since you were little, trying to do exactly what you're doing now ! You've tried to become the wife of your father and the mother of Orin ! You've always schemed to steal my place !" Of course Lavinia denies and resents these charges bitterly, but persists in her determination until her mother, in desperation, promises to send Brant away.

The return of General Mannon is indeed a strange homecoming. In Lavinia alone he finds genuine pleasure and affection. But he has determined, during his long years of facing death, to rediscover the secret of life and to break down, if possible, the barrier he has felt between himself and his wife, ever since the earliest days of their marriage. With great difficulty, he throws aside the re-

serve of years and tries to tell her of his loneliness and
his love. But he faces only the mocking mask of a woman
who has already determined that the only way to free
herself is to kill him. She has already arranged to have
Brant send her some poison tablets which she plans to
give her husband instead of the medicine his doctor has
prescribed for an increasing trouble of the heart. His
heart disease will explain his death to the world at large.
She and Adam will be free.

In the intimacy of their first night together, when Ezra
Mannon feels the false atmosphere of her pretended affection, she suddenly goads him with an open statement of
her love for Brant, and tells him, moreover, Brant's true
identity as one of the "outlawed" Mannons. The emotional strain brings on, as she had planned, a severe heart
attack. She substitutes for his medicine the poison Brant
has sent her. But in his death agony, Ezra Mannon calls
out for Lavinia who reaches his room just in time to see
him point an accusing finger at Christine and cry out "She's
guilty — not medicine!" This miscarriage of her plans
is too much for Christine. She faints before she can
conceal the package containing the poison tablets. Lavinia finds them, and at last, like the children of the
House of Atreus, knows the full measure of her mother's
guilt. The play ends with Lavinia's cry to the dead man,
"Father! Don't leave me alone! Come back to me!
Tell me what to do!"

In even the first part of this trilogy, one finds, of

course, innumerable links to the struggles of the past
which have beset the poet's imagination. The strength
of the Mannon family, for example, has come from the
sea. But it is also the sea, in the person of Captain Brant,
which helps to kill Ezra Mannon. Ezra, in his great
loneliness of soul, is not unlike any number of the lonely
souls, old and young, who wander through the stages of
the poet's long journey, seeking but never finding understanding and completion.

Christine herself is not of the Mannons. [She is the
unattainable "outsider" to those who love only themselves or the image of themselves. She can love Brant,
but only because, though part Mannon, he is the son of
another stock and, like herself, part outsider, "foreigner."
He is despised of the proud Mannons, because he comes
of a servant stock, and the Mannons can not serve others,
being without humility. [Outsiders are poison to the self-
love of the Mannons, much as Pompeia gave poison to
Miriam, the wife of Lazarus. Yet Christine is the
mother of the Mannon children, of those destined to
expiate the primal sin of the house. [That which kills is
also fated to be that which will bring new life, because it
comes from without the charmed and deadly circle of self-
love.] In this, the poet touches instinctively upon that
astounding [paradox of mankind's experience, that the redemption from man's self-love can be found only through
the death of man himself at the hands of what is itself
evil — the outsider, the Caligula, the Pompeia, evil, in

spite of itself, serving the ends of good. Even in that early play, "Bound East for Cardiff," this attitude of the poet toward death as a spiritual re-birth was the dominant theme. It comes back in the present tragedy, even under a hideous guise, to achieve its cleansing purpose in the soul ; the "Earth's transfigured birth-pain" of the "Great God Brown," out of which "the laughter of Man returns to bless and play again in innumerable dancing gales of flame upon the knees of God !"

Again, as in so many of O'Neill's plays, the point may be urged in criticism that the symbols chosen to express such profound instincts of the human soul are brutal in their morbidity, in their frequently perverted sensuality, or in the dimensions of their pride and arrogance. One might say, for example, in all deep reverence, and speaking intentionally in the narrowest limits of its significance, that the drama of Calvary caught up the universal experience of mankind in terms so lofty and so completely of the spirit, that any restatement of it in terms such as those of Greece, before Calvary, would amount to a catastrophe of human expression. One could point out that even the Greeks approached their climactic story of the soul with an almost Olympian detachment, and under the ægis of forces that lifted sin and retribution to proportions of philosophic sweep. The same could be said, in lesser degree, of Richard Wagner's recasting of Norse folk lore, whereas the Christian poets, such as the Catholic Dante or the Puritan Milton, held closely to the new dispensation of a spiritualized and exalted expression. (But here is precisely where O'Neill appears as the product of his generation — of that inner compulsion to create, which was part of the fibre of the nineties, of that growing materialism bred of the dark age of an overproud science which opened the twentieth century, of that increasing passion for realism which only expressed the hunger of souls deprived of spiritual vitality, of the increasing doubts and uncertainties and periods of black despair which the fiasco of man's scientific destruction of himself in the great war brought to pass.)

The true significance of O'Neill's poetic experience should not, in all charity, be measured by standards of the ages of great faith, before man experienced his destructive scientific love of himself, but should be taken rather in contrast with other contemporary products of his own age and habits of thought and modes of expression. The extraordinary quality of his work is not the brutality nor the ultra-realism of its expression but the inner content of that expression. It is almost paradoxical that he firmly chose as his themes problems of good and evil at the very time when his contemporaries were trying to abolish all distinction between good and evil. It is a matter of paramount interest that he always discovered tragedy as the invariable outcome of evil deeds and thoughts when the flippant (and desperate) spirit of his age found evil a convenient vehicle for comedy. It is of the essence of all of his work that he continued an undaunted quest of the high romance of spiritual truth, even in moods of utter darkness, when others were relaxing into cynicism and bitter indifference. If we accept a true poet as one who feels ahead of his times and carries within him something of the prophet, then the hunger and thirst of O'Neill for some sort of spiritual resolution of the mighty conflicts of the soul has a significance for the future of his generation which far outweighs the crude and often repellent quality of the symbols used in describing his quest. The symbols are part of the mood and temper of his times, and share their ugliness, but the poet's quest beneath the symbols is not only of other times but quite possibly of days still unborn.

The second part of the trilogy, "The Hunted," comprises the revenge of Lavinia and Orin for their father's murder. Orin returns from the hospital camp two days after the tragedy, while the body of Ezra Mannon is still laid out in his study. There is a subtle and terrific struggle between Lavinia and Christine for the control of Orin's weak will. Christine tries to mother him as of old, to play on his deep affection for her, and to warn him of the terrible charges he may hear from Lavinia. Christine tells him that Lavinia is really out of her mind. Intuitively, Orin feels a deep suspicion of his mother, but emotionally he can not bear to think any evil of her. Deep in his heart, he is almost relieved at his father's death, as he can now have his mother entirely to himself, and be as a child completely immersed in her love. During the long and murderous days of the war, he has often had the vision, as he killed men, that it was "like murdering the same man over and over" and as if "the man was myself !"   Their faces, he says, "keep coming back in dreams — and they change to Father's face — or to mine." To be rid of his father, and also of the man in himself, so that he could return to childhood in his mother's arms had become his half-conscious obsession.   He wants to be alone with his mother in the enchanted islands of his dreams, with the whole world apart from them.   Christine encourages this mood in the hope that it will make Orin her champion against Lavinia.

But Lavinia, with something of the severity of her dead father, holds him grimly to a realization of the truth. She makes him, in spite of himself, acknowledge his mother's guilt, and then, finding that that alone might not be enough to move him to vengeance, plays upon his instant jealousy of Brant.   The thought of another man claiming his mother's love is too much for him.   He and Lavinia secretly follow their mother to her rendezvous with Brant on his ship, in Boston harbor, and overhear her plans to escape.   When Christine has left, Orin enters Brant's cabin and kills him.   As he does so, the same old image of death comes before him.   It is as if he had again killed his father !

Orin and Lavinia return to the ancient house of Mannon to tell Christine what they have done.   Orin, immediately under her spell again, now that Brant is dead, begs

for her forgiveness. But it is too late. Christine goes
into the house and shoots herself. It is here that we find
the greatest departure from the Greek tragedy. The
Greek Orestes kills his mother to avenge his father. In
the O'Neill play, the mother kills herself, Orin remaining
to the last under the cloud of desire to have her protecting
arms about him. And then the new and final theme appears—the assumption by Lavinia of her mother's rôle.
She takes the bewildered Orin in her arms and whispers
soothingly to him, "You have me, haven't you? I love
you. I'll help you to forget." Thus Christine's accusa-
tion is justified, that Lavinia wished to take her place.

The third play, "The Haunted," begins a year later,
after Lavinia and Orin have completed a year's voyage to
China and the Far East. In the far land of Kublai Kaan
and the Princess Kukachin, a great change has taken place.
Lavinia has lost the stern angularity of former days, in
which she so closely resembled her father, and has become
strikingly like her mother. She even wears a dress of the
same green color her mother used to wear, instead of the
black she once affected. Orin, on the other hand, who
was formerly unable to hold the bearing of a soldier, now
carries himself woodenly erect. "His movements and
attitudes have the statue-like quality that was so marked
in his father. He now wears a close-cropped beard in
addition to his mustache, and this accentuates his resemblance to his father." The children are now living in
the ghosts of their parents.

Both Orin and Lavinia are aware of the change. In his moments of morbid bitterness, Orin even boasts of having become a Mannon and accuses Lavinia of having acquired a soul like his mother's, "as if you were stealing her — as if her death had set you free — to become her!" But Lavinia, in spite of welcoming the change in herself, cries out "What we need most is to get back to simple normal things and begin a new life"— a cry that was to become prophetic for the poet's own soul, when, later, the simple and tender beauty of "Ah, Wilderness!" was to unfold in his imagination. Lavinia tries sternly to make Orin face his haunting ghosts, to acknowledge fully to himself his mother's double guilt and her free choice of suicide. But the attempt is only partly successful.

A fresh touch of reality also comes into Lavinia's life through her friendship for Peter Niles, whom she has known since childhood. The thought of him has been growing in her mind during the long months of her voyage. The sea has had a cleansing effect upon her. "The ship and the sea — everything that was honest and clean" has reminded her of Peter. And another thought has come to her, too. "Remember I'm only half Mannon" she reminds Peter when they are at last together. The blood of the "outsider" has been doing its work, to give her a new strength to face life. She now wants to marry Peter. But the spectre of Orin comes between them — Orin who is still sick with the old guilt of the Mannons, "possessed by hate and death." Orin discovers

Lavinia kissing Peter, and jealousy seizes him. The woman who has taken the place of his mother can not be permitted to love another man!

Orin becomes a living terror for Lavinia. His increasing sense of guilt (for the indirect killing of his mother rather than for the murder of Brant, of course) makes him want to confess everything. He has allowed himself to become engaged to Peter's sister, Hazel Niles, but he is afraid to be alone with her, and Lavinia is afraid to have them alone together. His guilty conscience might make him confess. He is secretly preparing a written confession of his crime — and this Lavinia suspects rather than knows. She at last forces an admission from him, and then brother and sister lacerate each other with accusations. It is again as if the ghosts of Christine and Ezra were walking in the house. And then a deeper terror than the dread of Orin's confessing intervenes. In his growing insanity and in his jealous determination to prevent Lavinia from marrying Peter, Orin sees Lavinia as neither mother nor sister but as a woman, like the French-Canadian servant girl who was the mother of Brant. In an agony of revulsion and rage at this crowning revelation, Lavinia turns on Orin. "I wish you were dead!" she cries, "You're too vile to live! You'd kill yourself if you weren't a coward!"

Slowly the idea takes possession of Orin's deranged mind. In death he can join his mother. He will be able to ask her forgiveness. He will find peace. He starts to rush from the room. Lavinia makes an attempt to stop him, but at that moment Peter comes in, and Orin escapes to his father's study. Lavinia throws herself hysterically into Peter's arms, murmuring "no one has the right to keep anyone from peace!" Peter, alarmed, starts to go after Orin, but Lavinia holds him tightly to her and talks against time. There is the sound of a shot. Orin has killed himself. Lavinia is the last of the Mannons.

In the closing scene of the tragedy, after Orin's funeral, Lavinia is again in black. The resemblance to her mother has disappeared. She is filling the house with flowers for Peter, whom she feels she must marry. She must escape forever from the house of Mannon. But Hazel, Peter's sister, to whom Orin has hinted just enough to make her feel the terror of the Mannon story, comes to accuse Lavinia of the guilt of Orin's death and to plead with her to give up Peter. Lavinia is steadfast in her determination to marry him. But when he comes to her, she finds a growing suspicion and bitterness in his eyes. The dead are already standing between them. Almost in a frenzy, she asks him for his love, but even as she does so, the name of Adam, like the ghost of Adam Brant, escapes her lips. "I can't marry you, Peter," she cries in sudden defeat, "The dead are too strong!" And then, to drive him from her, she lies about herself. She takes a jealous word that Orin has dropped about a native in the far-off islands they had visited, and pretends the charge was true. As Peter leaves her, horror-struck, she calls after him that it was a lie. But her cry is too feeble, too defeated. He does not hear. Lavinia is alone again with the Mannon dead.

To Seth, the old gardener, Lavinia confides her last resolve. There is nothing left to do but return into the house. "Don't go in there, Vinnie!" he exclaims in superstitious fright. But she is grimly determined now. "Don't be afraid," she says, "I'm not going the way Mother and Orin went. That's escaping punishment. And there's no one left to punish me. I'm the last Mannon. I've got to punish myself! Living alone here with the dead is a worse act of justice than death or prison! I'll never go out or see anyone! I'll have the shutters nailed closed so no sunlight can ever get in. I'll live along with the dead, and keep their secrets, and let them hound me, until the curse is paid out and the last Mannon is let die." As she enters the house, to remain there in lifelong expiation, her movements become the wooden, angular embodiment of the Mannons.

There is still pride left in the soul of Lavinia, and a "strange cruel smile of gloating over the years of self-torture" on her face as she begins her penance. But above and beyond the words of the poet's description, there is the feeling of deepest introversion, of the turning back of the feminine soul into its innermost depths, as if to discover, in death to herself, the one last chance of a new life. Beneath the Mannon mask of utter love of self flows the blood of the "outsider," that which brought death to all the males of the fated line, but may still find in the woman a chance for re-birth. . . "What we need most is to get back to simple normal things and begin a new life." That was Lavinia's cry after feeling the cleansing of the sea.   One feels that in the deliberate, purposeful turning back into her past, Lavinia, the woman, unlike the frightened child-men who turned back to the maternal past, may discover the secret of living with fears until they are tamed, of opening her eyes to truth instead of mocking shadows, of finding tenderness in place of the sinister giants that seemed to block the agonizing path to maturity and peace.   This feeling, so different from the mask of self-torturing words that clothe it, was soon to be confirmed in that tender and compassionate play of youth, filled with understanding and friendly acceptance — in "Ah, Wilderness !", which proved, without the hideous masks of fear, to be, indeed, "paradise enow."

XXII

"AH, WILDERNESS!"

Reassurance

Two plays grew together from the deep purposeful turning back that closed the Electra tragedy. In one, "Days Without End," O'Neill sought directly, in surrender to Christ crucified, a truth that would set him free. But it must have been a difficult play to write. There were four versions of it in all, and between the second and third versions, as if something had to be done to clear the path, he wrote "Ah, Wilderness!" easily and joyously in a few weeks' time. After that, he was able to complete the play of deeper spiritual conflict.

This apparently innocent and tender little comedy of adolescence is really much more important than it seems in the poet's unconscious scheme of things. It marked an end to that terrible fear which had made every symbol of youth appear like some hideous monster. It was unquestionably the beginning of a third and entirely new period in O'Neill's creative life, the period of full manhood of the soul. The early adolescent period, which ended with "All God's Chillun Got Wings," was full of a hyper-consciousness of divided personality and of quick responsiveness through feeling to outward circumstance. It was also full of the inhibited desire to create, and of the welling pride of untamed youth. Timidity and self-abasement were there, too. The second period covered the difficult gulf between adolescence and maturity. To become a man was imperative, yet the protected days of childhood, with love confined to one's self and to one's immediate family, seemed softly alluring. Until those ties could be broken, they became like sinister demons which had to be killed. It was the folk lore stage, filled with dragons and dying gods. It corresponded fully to Wagner's Siegfried period, with a touch of Nietzsche's Zarathustra thrown in for good measure in the passionate exultation of Lazarus. But the killing of the Mannons was a twilight of these old gods. Valhalla, and the bridge back to it, were burned. The time had come for the Parsifal motif, and the healing of the old wound of Amfortas.

But before this could be done, it was necessary to take a reassuring backward look — just to make certain that the demons and dragons had vanished. "Ah, Wilderness !" was the result of that look — a vision of youth and parents and young love with all the hideous masks thrown away — a mother who was just a kindly, humor-

ous, plump middle-aged woman who still remembered her
own youth and romance ; brothers who teased each other
and boasted a bit and thought and acted differently,
but did not by any manner of means drain each other's
lives and strength away ; a young girl one loved and had
lovers' quarrels with occasionally, but not in the least like
a poisonous "outsider"; and, above all else, a father who
was shrewd, tender-hearted, loyal and deeply understanding, a father whom one could kiss at rare intervals with
deep affection and thankfulness. The stern Ephraim
Cabot turned out to be nothing more than lovable Nat
Miller, the best father a boy could have. The mocking,
impish Caligula melted quietly into Uncle Sid who loved
his bottle a bit too much and could be uproariously funny
when drunk. The wilderness of devouring dragons became, at a glance, paradise enough for anyone !

It is interesting to remember how civilization itself has
made just such delightful discoveries. Poets, after all,
do seem to act like small cross sections of mankind. The
whole western world was under a spell of terrifying gods
when the long night of Europe first set in. Hideous
figures, half men, half beasts, lurked in every Roman
garden when Caligula was crying for blood. The shadow
of Pan fell on every field and hill. Then the words of a
parable began to fall like the rain of a new flood —"he
that humbleth himself shall be exalted." Through centuries, this rain fell, and to many the heavens probably
seemed dark, but the rain was washing the fields and the

gardens clean. As the light came forth again in the twelfth and thirteenth centuries, a Francis Bernardone, standing on his beloved hills of Umbria, could find a clean and free brotherhood with nature. There was no disfiguring shadow of a monster across the sunfilled valleys. Man could come back to nature loving and unafraid.

There is something of this same significance to the simple, unaffected realism and tender affection of "Ah, Wilderness!" The play does little more than tell the story of two days in the lives of a small-town Connecticut family during the first decade of this century. Nat Miller is a newspaper proprietor who comfortably harbors within his house his own sister, his wife's brother and a brood of children ranging from ten up to college age. Richard Miller, with two older brothers, a sister of about his own age and a younger brother, is in the adolescent throes of reading Swinburne, the Rubaiyat, Bernard Shaw and Ibsen, and of being in love with Muriel, a crotchety neighbor's daughter. The crotchety neighbor believes a boy who reads such "stuff" is a bad influence for a young girl, and forces her to write a letter breaking off her "engagement" to Richard. This plunges the ardent youngster into a fit of Ibsenesque despair. An older college boy, thinking him older in the way of the world than he is, suggests a "night out," which Richard boastfully agrees to, "just to show" his heartless lady-love how little he cares. But he does not succeed in doing much more than get very sick on two strong drinks and in having an itinerant lady's advances fall flat before the image of Muriel still stoutly entrenched in his mind.

Nat Miller, however, feels in fatherly duty bound to give Richard some sound advice. Probably no scene between father and son has ever been more tenderly written than the one in which Nat tries to tell Richard how to avoid the dangers of life without seeming to encourage him in courting those dangers. He does not know, until the painfully embarrassed scene is over, that Richard and Muriel have found a way to break all parental obstacles and are once more in the seventh heaven of "Youth's sweet scented manuscript." But Richard understands what his father has been trying to do. When they say good night, Richard turns impulsively and kisses his father — and then hurries out onto the porch to watch the moon set on his day of love. Nat Miller turns to his wife and says huskily: "First time he's done that in years. I don't believe in kissing between fathers and sons after a certain age — seems mushy and silly — but that meant something! And I don't think we'll ever have to worry about his being safe — from himself — again. And I guess no matter what life will do to him, he can take care of it now."

Quite aside from the general importance of "Ah, Wilderness!" as marking a new phase and a new attitude in O'Neill's work, there is a very special significance in the emphasis laid on the father and son relationship. It is the first O'Neill play in which the father has not been a pale, stiff shadow, like Ezra Mannon, or a narrow, stern object of hate and jealousy, like Ephraim Cabot. Earlier plays have all stressed the maternal side, either in longing or in "sinister" dread. What the sudden tender understanding in "Ah, Wilderness!" amounts to is nothing less than the development of the full grown man in the poet's own make up, of a man willing and eager to take up creative responsibility in life and able at last to see his own father as another individual, respected and apart, loved and admired and — no longer an object of jealousy. Only the complete breaking of the mental tie to childhood could give this new freedom. The old gods of fearsome imagination are dead. Truth can be looked in the face, without fear, and with love.

In a curious but quite logical sense, "Ah, Wilderness!" is like a second "Strange Interlude"— except that it is not strange, but blessedly familiar. It is a taking stock of things just as "Strange Interlude" was, but in a wholly different mood. It is a glance of mature recognition and acceptance, rather than a pained and terrified searching into fearsome depths. O'Neill might have moved directly into the theme of "Days Without End," and did actually make the effort to do so. But the writing first of "Ah, Wilderness!" became as necessary as opening the windows in a stuffy room before beginning new work after a storm. We must remember that the shutters of the House of Mannon were nailed up tight! The house needed fresh air and sunshine to dispel the ghosts of the past completely. Lavinia Mannon had said : "What we need most is to get back to simple normal things and begin a new life." Lavinia was speaking for the poet himself. She was right — and she was also prophetic.

XXIII

"DAYS WITHOUT END"

Victory in Surrender

With the fresh air of "Ah, Wilderness!" beating upon his temples, O'Neill was at last able to complete the third and then the fourth and final version of "Days Without End." It was the first play to be wholly of the third stage which his poetic imagination was now entering. Like "Dynamo," it suffers somewhat from over-intensity and from a certain sense of strangeness, like a wanderer finding himself in a new and unfamiliar land. But "Days Without End" is a play of splendid affirmation instead of death. It is a play of a man's problem in the full surge of real life. It is also a play of victory through the great mystical paradox of surrender. In other words, it has all the qualities one would expect in the new phase of spiritual manhood, including the weaknesses, the excess of zeal and the faltering steps in a strange land without well marked trails.

"Days Without End" is the story of John Loving — a man divided against himself. O'Neill uses two stage characters to express a single person, the real John, and

his other masked self, Loving. But there is a distinct
difference between this use of the mask and its use in
former plays such as the "Great God Brown." Loving is
not a mask symbolizing John's present attitude to the
world. He is not a symbol of concealment and false
attitude, but very much a symbol of the past, of an older
self. The other characters in the play are not aware of
the existence of this old self. When Loving speaks, in
bitterness or derision, the others think it is John himself
speaking. At the culmination of the play, when John
surrenders to the spirit of Christ crucified, Loving dies,
defeated, and John becomes a single unified self at last,
John Loving, radiant in his victory over the old self. In
earlier plays, the mask was triumphant and killed the real
man. Now victory belongs to the man and it is the mask
that dies.

John is married to Elsa, a woman to whom fidelity in
marriage is of the utmost importance. She left a former
husband as soon as she discovered that he was unfaithful
to her. We do not know whether the former husband is
alive or dead. He is mentioned merely as a symbol and
proof of her attitude. She considers marriage "a true
sacrament" with high and imperative obligations, and is
happy in the belief that she has discovered in John a man
who wholly shares her feelings. John, for his part, has
found in Elsa's love the end of a long and weary road,
upon which he has traversed every phase of self-torture
and doubt, and every phase of temporary belief, from

strident atheism through socialism and communism and the quietude of the Far Eastern philosophies.   None of the "isms" has satisfied his soul, nor succeeded in calming his fear of life.   But at last, in Elsa's love, he has found what seems to him completion.   It is not hard to see in the former John the poet of all the earlier plays, now come into his own in a love and marriage of the real world — a marriage that makes demands upon him which he must face as a full grown man.

But the old self, Loving, still hovers about.   His mask is described as having the look of death, but it still shadows John like an echo of the past.   It makes him fearful of his new-found happiness.   With a perversity which poets have understood for centuries, it makes him want to kill the very thing he loves.   And it has partly succeeded. On one occasion, John, goaded by Loving, has committed the sin of adultery, not in the weakness of overwhelming passion, but in a fit of sudden defiant cruelty.   The woman, Lucy Hillman, with whom he has shared this guilt, was seeking only revenge on her dissolute husband. But in her passion for this revenge and in John's insane feeling that he must kill the spirit of the love that had brought him too much happiness, the extremes have met. The memory of this bears down on John with an oppressive sense of guilt.   He has good reason to believe that Elsa will neither understand nor forgive.   Yet he can not bear the thought of living a lie.   The memory of his sin comes between him and Elsa and poisons the very perfection he seeks.

As the play starts, John is trying to find a way of discovering, before he confesses, whether Elsa could possibly understand the strange contradiction of soul that led to his infidelity. He is writing his own story in the form of a novel which he intends to read to Elsa as a test. In the midst of this work, his uncle, a Catholic priest from the Middle West, arrives at John's office. Something has made Father Baird feel that John needs him. It is from their intimate talk of former days that we learn of John's past struggles. The priest, tolerant with the wisdom of centuries, is not a stern voice of conscience. But he knows that John's weakness has come from placing all his faith in human love alone, that he needs, for his inner strength, a return to the faith of his youth. John, too, knows this instinctively. But the voice of the masked Loving intervenes. The kindly advice of the priest is met now by John with humble acceptance, and now with bitter mockery by Loving. To Father Baird, there is only one person in the room, but to the audience there are the two men fighting each other.

Not the least interesting part of this dual concept is the use of the name, Loving, for the mask of the old diabolic self. Perhaps the best explanation of this apparent paradox is to be found in the poet's earlier plays. It is the loving side of the man that has sinned the most against the integrity of the soul — sinned in loving false gods and in the incest symbol of self-love. That which might have been all beauty has become the beast because it has loved itself rather than something greater than and outside of itself. This would also explain the end of the play, that in surrender to Christ, the false loves die and the loving side of John is reborn to new life. John finds himself in surrendering himself.

John's plan of using his novel to test Elsa's understanding and forgiveness does not work out, due to a series of happenings. Lucy, feeling the need of talking to someone, comes to Elsa, and without mentioning names, tells of what she had done in seeking revenge. Thus, when John reads the outline of his novel to Elsa and to Father Baird, who passes the evening with them, Elsa recognizes it at once as his own story and not fiction. Moreover, the voice of Loving keeps breaking through in cold cynicism and defiance, expressing a secret wish that Elsa might die and thus relieve John from the need of confession. John's own father and mother had both died of pneumonia when he was a boy of fourteen. His loss of faith had dated from that early tragedy — much as Dion Anthony's loss of faith started with the external cruelty of Billy Brown. Now the spirit of Loving prompts him, against all his better instincts, to wish a similar death for Elsa. If death took his first love, his parents from him, why not his last love as well ? John, impelled by his demon, suggests the death of the wife as the probable end of his unfinished novel. Elsa listens in horror. She has only just recovered from influenza, and knows the danger of a relapse. Does John really wish her death? Has his infidelity to their love and to their whole ideal of marriage driven him to this? There is a wintry storm outside. She leaves John and Father Baird, and rushes out into the night.

When Elsa returns, the fever has come upon her. The cruel design of Loving is about to work itself out as a tragic reality in John's life. Days of illness pass, and the crisis arrives. Elsa still can not forgive, though John has pleaded with her for understanding. She has lost the desire for life that might bring her through the crisis. A terrific spiritual battle begins between John and Loving, with Father Baird calling upon John to turn to prayer. Loving mocks. Prayer to the God who took John's parents from him? But Father Baird persists. Prayer alone can give him back Elsa's love and forgiveness and perhaps her life. At last, with the shadow of his old self trying to block the way, John rushes forth to the church where he prayed as a child, and there, before the figure of Christ on the Cross, he asks the help of the Son of Man — the One Whom, in all these years, he could never forgive for taking the love of his parents from him. But now the spirit of loving surrender comes back to him. "Why hast Thou forsaken me?" he cries out, "O Brother Who lived and suffered and died with us, Who knoweth the tortured hearts of men, canst Thou not forgive—

now — when I surrender all to Thee — when I have forgiven Thee — the love Thou once took from me !" As
John calls out to Christ, the figure of Loving stands
defiantly before the Cross.

There is a moment of darkness, and then, slowly, a
light, as from the great Crucifix, seems to illuminate John.
He feels the warmth of Christ's love and forgiveness in
his heart. His face becomes radiant. "I am forgiven !"
he cries, "I can forgive myself — through Thee ! I can
believe ! . . . At last I see ! I have always loved ! O
Lord of Love, forgive Thy poor blind fool !" And then
it is that Loving, too, cries out "Thou hast conquered,
Lord. Thou art — the End. Forgive — the damned
soul — of John Loving !," and, as he utters these words,
falls forward dead. But the poet tells us that "John
Loving — he, who had been only John — remains standing with his arms stretched up to the Cross, an expression
of mystic exaltation on his face. The corpse of Loving
lies at the foot of the Cross, like a cured cripple's testi-
monial offering in a shrine." Father Baird comes upon
John thus, and starts to tell him that Elsa has passed the
crisis and that her first words were forgiveness for John.
But John already knows this in his heart. He turns to
Father Baird, his face aglow with new love and faith.
"Life laughs with God's love again !" he cries, "Life
laughs with love !" John has indeed become John
Loving, the symbol of the loving John finding life at the
foot of the Cross.

It must remain for later plays, still unwritten, to tell us what John Loving in the poet's soul will do to meet the tasks of the manhood of his spirit. In every age of a poet's experience there are battles to be fought. Faith may ride the storms unharmed and walk upon the waves of new terrors. But the storms themselves succeed the calms in never ending rhythm, and a Peter, striding upon the heaving waters, may have to call again for help as faith wavers, even for an instant. "Days Without End" is not the final peace-filled consummation of a Parsifal raising the Grail. It is more the young Parsifal seizing the spear cast by Klingsor, standing exaltedly before the withering of the magic gardens, but still with the long road of knighthood and of test to travel. Perhaps the poet's Amfortas still lies in the Graalsburg, sick of his old wound. The spear must be brought to touch his side. Kundry, like the weakened body of Elsa, must be brought to new life in the purifying beauty of a Good Friday spell.

These tasks, one feels, are still ahead. Each poet brings them before us in different array. For Wagner it was the story of the Grail. To Francis Thompson, it was the Hound of Heaven. To Milton, it was Paradise Lost and Regained. To Dante, it was the spirit of Beatrice, leading him to the vision of "the Love that moves the sun and all the stars." But between the experiences of all the great poets, there is an inner unity more profound than the mere symbols of their imagination. In just what symbols Eugene O'Neill will describe the further stages of his journey, no one, not even the poet himself, can foretell. They will undoubtedly spring from the stirring and uneasy civilization of which he is a part. They will surely give forth a rumor of discoveries still to be made by other men of his own times. That is of the very essence of the poet's task. We can only wish him well in the burden of his days ahead, knowing that the inner spirit which has driven him thus far on a dark and painful road can not and will not desert him as he nears the climax of the poet's quest.